DUST IN MY EYES

A Collection of Poems and Sketches

Christopher P. McClure

Dust in My Eyes
ISBN: 978-1-946180-41-4
© 2023 by Christopher P. McClure
BarMPublishing@gmail.com

Cover and Text Design: Lisa Simpson
SimpsonProductions.net

ACKNOWLEDGMENTS

Many people have influenced me or aided me in the development and completion of this book. The first to interest me in poetry was "Cotton" Lewis. Many years ago, he persistently insisted that I "keep on writing." The "challenge" to start a blog came from an uncle, Cecil Oursbourn. He knew I needed the challenge.

Several friends have not only inspired some of these posts, but unknowingly suggested ideas that found their way into a poem – in particular, Neal Odom. My son, Cache, and daughter Cimarron have both inspired me at various times as well as having dealt with my moodiness when inspiration or "quiet" was a struggle. Betty Jo Gigot has been a constant source of encouragement. I also would like to thank Jim Whitt for his encouragement and his reference for Lisa Simpson who has been invaluable in preparing the book for printing. My parents, Carl and Helen McClure, who encouraged me to read widely and to write clearly and concisely, also deserve recognition.

Last, but by far most important, is my wife Missy who has continued to encourage me as well as to help with the editing and revisions. She deserves a medal for putting up with my moodiness.

DEDICATION

For my family.

INTRODUCTION

This book is the result of a challenge received back in 2007, when my uncle pushed me to begin a Blog.

The original blog was called Panhandle Poetry and Other Thoughts which can still be found on the Internet. It includes prose as well as poetry. Many of the poems found in this book were published there, but not all. Some have been modified for various reasons – mainly that they were written hurriedly and contained mistakes of one form or fashion.

As I began to develop this book, I realized that some of the poems needed clarification. That is what first led me to include illustrations and, in some cases, a brief paragraph or so of additional information. The illustrations have presented their own challenges since my artistic talent is poorly developed. Some may be a bit clumsy or amateurish in appearance. It is not my intent to provide polished works of art, merely illustrations that push the mind into areas that might not be stimulated by the words alone.

With a few exceptions, the drawings are from photographs taken by family members or me. In many cases they are specific to the words, but in others, they are merely page fillers. Is that such a bad thing? There is a lot of white space left when my goal of a single poem per page is met. The illustrations fill space. That gives them purpose and purpose is a good thing to have! (Just ask Jim Whitt.)

Some of the poems in this work are meant to be humorous while others are simply observations of everyday life. Frequently, nature has been my inspiration and you will find a few creatures sprinkled through that are often overlooked in our day-to-day existence. There also are poems that are meant to inspire thought. Some may appear to be subtly political in nature, but they also are meant to point out things that require some consideration rather than blind adherence to dogma.

Finally, poetry is a somewhat nebulous thing. You will hear rhythms in some but not in others. The meters will vary and sometimes fail to exist. I have simply expressed the thoughts of a moment in time in some fashion – simply, or playfully depending on the mood.

I hope you enjoy.

THE RURAL LIFE

SHADOWS DANCING IN THE GRASS

Rhythmic thunder of pounding hooves
Fades into the heartbeats
Thrumming in my head
As the swinging loop gathers speed.
The dun stallion nipping at the harem flanks
Is defiant of my threat.
His focus is protection
While I seek convergence.
The moment stretches
As the nylon snake sails forth
To be foiled by a puff of wind
Which sends the shadows
Dancing in the grass.
Only dust remains.

THE LIGHTHOUSE

Shaped by the hand of time,
The Lighthouse stands.
The enduring symbol of the Palo Duro,
The Lighthouse stands.
Through the ravages of wind and rain,
The Lighthouse stands.
Despite the touch of man,
The Lighthouse stands.
May we each stand as
The Lighthouse stands.

"Therefore, put on the full armor of God, so that when the day of evil comes, you may be able to stand your ground, and after you have done everything, to stand." – Ephesians 6:13 (NIV)

JOHN

Standing about six-foot-five plus two inches of boot heel
if you stood him up straight,
John is topped by a black felt hat that's pulled down tight
Because he doesn't like to chase it in the wind.

Unless otherwise occupied,
his thumbs stay hooked in his pants pockets
Because there's not much else to do with 'em
when he's talking to someone.
It used to be he always had a ready smile
for just about everyone that came his way,

But the cares of trying to build his own herd have
Made that smile so scarce you sometimes wonder
if his favorite dog just died.
His face is lined with years that age him faster
than the calendar or his friends from school

That went on to city jobs because the pay was better
and the work wasn't nearly so hard.
John's a survivor, made from the stock that built
this Western country from scratch

Way back before the
roads or the fences cut it
into nice, neat patches
that called it tamed.
He's an anachronism
living a life that many a
youngster once dreamed
of living

Before reality crashed
and sent them scurrying for safety and security.

Loneliness and wind and too much sun
have left their mark on this man

That was born at least a hundred years after his allotted slot in
The ribbon of time had expired.

GLOBAL WARMING

Bundled from head to toe he climbs into Ole Red.
The frigid blast has brought more snow
and his mind is filled with dread.
It has been a tough winter for ranchers on the Plains.
The drifts are deep and just won't melt
until the coming of spring rains.
He takes an axe to break the ice then climbs back into his truck
And sticks his hands up to the heater to try and warm them up.
Backing up his bale fork to the lined-up rolls of hay,
He's looking forward to the coming of a nice warm summer day.

The cows need extra feed for calving will come soon.
He hopes they don't start coming for at least another moon.
As he's plowing across the prairie in his worn-out, trusty Red,
He's thankful that he has this bunch of cows that must be fed.
He thinks about his calling and the life he might have chose
Instead of out here feeding cattle with hands and toes near froze.
He knows he didn't fit the life of city or, of town
So, he keeps on with his feeding as the snow is falling down.

He thinks about the craziness that some folks just confuse
About politics and genders and stuff that's in the news.
He knows there's things worth fighting for like life and liberty
And making sure the ones he loves are safe makes him think of family.
He just can't understand why there is so much hate-filled strife
When he just wants to
get on with his simple
life. He prays for protec-
tion that his kids might
feel no harm
And wonders about
this thing called global
warming when he just
wants to get warm.

SUBURBAN CREEP

In the early morning mist
The red-orange orb hangs
Suspended just above the
Purple-blue outline of the
Ancient walnut tree whose
Bare branches droop tiredly
Over the grazing cattle.
Whistling wings of Mallards
Rise from the broken surface
Of the once glassy pond
To soar above the thinning vapors
As they flee the night-fears,
Seeking their sustenance
Among the skeletal remains
Of last summer's bumper crop.
Broken by the barking of a
Farmer's watchful friend,
The stillness gives way to
Sounds of motors running,
Tires humming, children calling,
And life returning to the
Hectic pace of another day.

Rural Commuter

There's not much left of the old place now;
The house is there no more.
Junk equipment lies in piles
Where corrals once stood before.
The windmill tower is still in place
But the wheel and rod aren't there.
Nothing but a stump is left
Of the gnarled and ancient Pear.
The old stock tank can still be seen
Piled high with baling wire.
Where once there was an apple tree
Is now a worn out tire.
The garden's just a patch of weeds;
The chicken coop's caved in.
Where once stood a Quonset barn
Is twisted, rusted tin.
The old home place just ain't the same
As it was in days of old,
The remains have lost their life it seems
It now feels gray and cold.
The neighbor's farms are changing too
With houses all run down
And weeds have taken over everything
Since they all moved into town.
The farmers have all left the farm;
They all just moved away.
Most prefer the city life
And commute to work each day.

CHIVALRY IS NOT DEAD

Chivalry is not dead.
It lives on in those who think there is truly a cowboy way.
It resides in a land of ma'am and sir.
It is the removed hat.
It is opening a door for the ladies.
It is almost humorous in its expression sometimes
Because it is filled with myth
And with a feigned humility that covers a pride with
Little tolerance for those who would be pretenders.
It is a club with initiation rites as intricate as the most arcane
Fraternity rituals.
It is a seeming backwardness steeped in knowledge gained
Through a lifetime of learning by watching the "old hands"
And from the hard knocks of
"Been there, done that."
It echoes the sounds of the deepest Ozarks,
The Texas Plains,
And the feedlots of Kansas.
It is at home in the high mountain valleys
Or on a western Indian Reservation.
It is heard in Elko, Billings, Brush,
Dodge, Kearney, Muleshoe,
Snowflake, Socorro, Gonzales,
And a thousand other towns and communities
Interspersing the landscape from the Mississippi
To the Pacific and from
The Valley to the Canadian North.
It lives on in all of its confused
And colorful expression, in the hearts
More than the mannerisms, of the
Modern mounted warriors
Who cling to the mistaken idea that toughness
Is shown only in physical endurance,
Hard drinking, and extreme living.
Contradictions abound.

OLD TOM

The jingle gives him away when he walks in the door;
He rarely arrives unheralded.
On a kid you might think it was for "show" but the spurs in this case
Were a natural part of the handmade boots they adorned.
The hair is thin on the top of his head but, rarely is it ever seen
For the paper-thin covering so yellow with grease that it is
Almost transparent except for the crust that has turned to
Permanent decoration in the vicinity of the hatband.
The holes in the crown were made with a knife
to let the heat escape as it should.
The stampede string that drapes from the back is worn to the point
That some pony's tail will soon be missing a few strands
To be plaited back in by the fingers that are gnarled and scarred
By too many years of working the livestock that is his life.
Fluent in Spanish and English alike,
he has worked the ranges from Argentina to Canada.
The wildest, he said, was the time he was shot down in a Piper Cub
Over the jungles of Uruguay by a band of guerrillas.
It seems they had been raiding stock from the spread
he was hired to patrol
By a corporate owner in New York City.
I asked if that meant he was a mercenary to which he replied,
"No, I was just the company troubleshooter."
Tom was once known in the outback of Paraguay
as that Christian Cowboy
Because he never failed to conduct a Sunday Service
in his humble home
Which was open to all comers at any time.
His son once told me that he had made more money than
most people will ever see in a lifetime
But gave it all away because he couldn't survive
without helping those in need.
The first time I saw him I felt sorry for this man
who was wearing a worn-out shirt
That had been patched at least a dozen times.
I suspected he was a down-and-out drifter that couldn't hold a job

And probably didn't have a nickel to his name.
The next time I saw him
He was sitting in a pickup with a laptop making entries
into a program he had written
That could tell you in detail anything anyone
would ever want to know
About the operation for which he was responsible.
It seems that he had written his Masters Thesis over "cell grazing"
Back in the days before the concept had seen the light
of any other researcher's eyes.
This Aggie was living the life that he loved
and loving the life that he lived
Because he never lost sight of his calling.
I'm proud to have called him my friend.

Ghosts of the Plains

Out on the wild prairie where tumbleweeds roll
and the dust-devils play in the sun,
There rode a young cowboy all hell-bent for leather,
and high in his hand was a gun.
The shimmering heat made him look like a specter
as he came flying over a rise.
The cloud of his dust looked just like a smudge
on the blue of the West Texas skies.
Suddenly, behind him there rose a wild band
of Kiowas quick on his heel.
The arrows were flying, the horse fell to earth,
and fear rent the air from his squeal.
The valiant young cowboy lay down 'hind his mount
and thunder spoke forth from his gun.
His Colt took a toll on the redskins that day
as they fell 'neath the hot Texas sun.
With blood streaming down he fought to the last
while the sun slowly sank from the sky.
When the fiery orb painted dark red the horizon
both day and young cowboy did die.
So were the dreams of my youth as I hunted
for arrowheads out on the Draw.
With visions so vivid I touched each found point;
it could only be ghosts that I saw.
(Previously published in The Territorial magazine.)

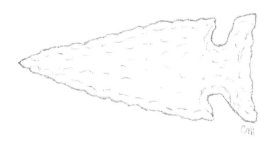

THE MISHAP

I had an old cow with a bad cancer eye
That I hauled into town to the Vet.
She was wild as a jackrabbit on a warm day
And could outrun a horse you can bet.

I pulled through the unloading area out back;
A new kid was running the gate.
We opened the trailer and the cow jumped right out
Blowin' snot and bellerin' her hate.

With considerable proddin' and a little finesse
She was headed right into the squeeze.
But the kid on the headgate missed with the catch
And the old gal was gone with the breeze.

She couldn't get far 'cause the gates had been shut
And the place was designed for such things.
When lo and behold from the west end of the barn
We heard some terrified screams.

It seems the receptionist, much to her surprise,
Had opened the door from up front
And come face-to-face with a one-eyed mad cow
Of whose rage she might be the brunt.

She threw all the papers that she had been carrying
And jumped into an empty stall.
Just as you would guess, she left the door open
And the cow ran into the hall.

She charged right into the front waiting room;
By then Doc was close on her tail,
But the lady who sat there with the manicured poodle
Suddenly began to turn pale.

The poodle jumped up and crawled under the chair
But the lady was frozen with terror.
Doc had to work fast so he grabbed the cow's tail;
He knew there was no margin for error.

Well, the tail did the trick and the cow spun around
And sent Doc flyin' up through the air.
Then that old Hereford cow jumped over the counter
And smashed flat the front office chair.

Our luck finally turned 'cause the cow saw her opening
And headed back out of the door.
Doc started tendin' to the sweet poodle lady
Who had fainted and fell to the floor.

We caught the old cow and Doc took her bad eye
Then began to clean up the mess.
That the kid who had first let the cow get away
Was concerned for his job, you can guess.

I loaded my cow after paying the bill
Which was only the standard fee.
Doc said, "There was nothing unusual about it
It's just a normal day's work for me."

THE OLD HOUSE

A wheat field
Covers the ground where
Once stood
A house.
The house
Was built around
The turn of the last
Century
From cast blocks
Hauled by wagon
From the nearest
Town.
It withstood tornados
And hail storms
And the
Dust Bowl.
It was thought to be
Haunted when
I was young.
The ghosts were
Raccoons.
My great grandmother
Was born in that
House.
They both are gone
Except in
Memory.

SPRING WORKS

Roping and dragging
Aren't common these days.
The ranchers have all
Gone to more modern ways.
They gather the cattle
On four-wheelers now
Instead of the way
Their grandfathers knew how.
They say that it's progress
And that it is smart.
But I think the old ways
Were a work of art.

SWEET ICED TEA

Sweet, iced tea
Is my drink of choice.
I want it brewed,
Not instant.

It needs to be cold!
If it is fresh brewed,
I like a glass full of ice
Then add tea and stir it

So the ice will melt
And cool it.
It's even better
Refrigerated.

Some folks think
That tea should be hot;
They speak of Earl Grey
And other varieties.

While I don't mind
A hot cup upon occasion,
I still prefer it iced
And very sweet.

Sweet, iced tea
And cornbread
And beans
Speak country –

Southern country.
Nothing cools you quicker
Than an ice cold glass
Of sweet, iced tea.

THE PEOPLE, NOT THE LAND

What seems a simple question
Is actually quite complex;
It is one that each should give some thought
Although it might well vex.

The question is what led you
To the land where you now live?
What brought you to this wondrous place
That takes the time you give?

My answer starts with ancestors
Of hardy pioneer stock
Who came out west in earlier times
Than this in which we walk.

My roots reach out to Scotland
Through Georgia and Oklahoma
And from Virginia through Kentucky
And the Ozarks of Missouri.

Each branch eventually converging
On these Plains of endless view
Where to my young parents
Came me, brand spanking new.

I grew up here on these open plains
That stretch as far as eye can see.
I grew to love the emptiness
That made me feel so free.

But then I left and went to school
In a very different place.
It was down in Central Texas
Where I was just another face.

I missed the wind – it never blew.
I felt smothered by humidity.
And almost everyone I met
Had grown up in a city.

I felt pressed upon at every turn
Like sardines in a can.
I needed space to get away
Where I could breathe again.

And so upon my settling down
I came back to the plains
And started a family
In this land of infrequent rains.

Eventually, as time went by,
My work made me to move
First to Kansas and then the city
Where I never found my groove.

From Dallas to Nebraska,
We packed our things once more.
Then finally back to Texas,
We set foot on friendly shore.

We were home. All was well.
It felt right again you see.
We live here now because
It's where God means for us to be.

It's not the open spaces
Or the wind that ever blows
That makes this Panhandle
The place where our heart grows.

It's the people, it's the family,
It's the friendly open hand
Of the folks that are life's blessing.
It's the people, not the land.

CULTIVATING COTTON

A handful of soil trickles through his fingers
As he looks across the ground
So recently covered by the massive
John Deere tractor and plow.
Squatting on one heel
He digs into the loose soil,
Testing the moisture
And the depth of the cultivation.
A smile creases the weathered face
As he heads back
To the pickup,
Cellphone pressed to his ear,
Directing one of the hired hands
On which field to cover next.
The squares are forming
And the promise of a good fall is heightened
By gentle rains that have fallen.
If it doesn't hail
And there's not an early freeze
And nothing breaks down
He might make a little money this year.
The banker will appreciate that.
They aren't too happy
When you must carry the note over
Into the new crop year.
Let's hope the price holds.

BOB

Bob is a cattleman
Who ranches west of town.
He's one of those on whom
You rarely see a frown.

If you need a volunteer
To get a project done
Immediately you think
That Bob is the one

To put in charge because
That's where you normally find
Him. Taking kids to camp
Or doing something kind

For one of the older folks
In town who can't quite
Get around much anymore.
Or if you watch you might

Catch him on a Sunday
Heading to Amarillo
For the prison ministry
Where he's a regular fellow

Sharing with those
Who need someone to care
In a dark place
Where many won't dare

To be seen. And if
There's a church cookout
He's the one to volunteer
To bring his grill out

And spend all day cooking
So the folks can enjoy
A wonderful meal
Cooked by this good old' boy.

Yep, Bob's a good friend
Who gets much out of life.
He has a couple of kids
And a loving wife.

He can play the drums
Or ride his "bike" with chrome spokes,
But he seems to be happiest
Helping out other folks.

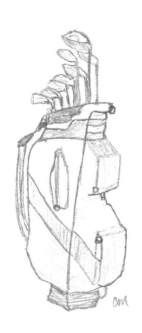

HARVEST TIME

Harvest time
Combines
Piles of grain
Changing leaves
Pumpkins
Scarecrows
Cool mornings
New wheat springing
Rural towns bustling
Football
Kids in school
Hurry in the air
Fruits of summer's labor
Before the winter rest.

HOME AWAY FROM HOME

A one-ton club-cab pickup
Parked out front of Joe's café
Guarded by a surly pup
That keeps the world at bay.

A thirty-thirty on a rack
That hangs behind the seat
Almost covered by spare tack
Just thrown in, none too neat.

A brass spittoon sits on the dash
That years back held a shine
But now is filled with moldering mash
And covered up with grime.

Sale receipts and tally sheets
Are piled up here and there;
Flyers from the auction meets
Just thrown in without care.

A stray left glove lays on the floor
Among the ground-in dirt
With empty snuff can lids galore
And a once-clean extra shirt.

The left rear fender's dented in,
The imprint of a cow
Who battled rope but didn't win
And into it did plow.

Speckled mud from grill to ball
This master of the road
Never even threats to stall
While pulling heavy load.

Lived-in, sure, and much abused,
Made for one to roam.
O'er many a hard mile it has cruised,
This cowboy's second home.

CHANGING MINDSET

Rocking horses,
Stick horses,
Shetland ponies,
Led rides,
Finally, in the saddle on my own.

Roy Rogers,
John Wayne,
Jimmy Stewart,
Clint Eastwood,
Said I'd be a cowboy when I'm grown.

Then one day my grandfather said to me,
"You don't want to be a cowboy.
You need to reach higher.
I was once a broke cowboy but then realized,
What I really wanted to be was a Cow Man."

High school,
College classes,
Raising kids,
Life happens.
Still, I kept on working for the dream.

Finally reached
Turning point;
Bought land
Good cows
Felt I'd finally earned the Cow Man's hat.

Then one day a Realtor came by
And said, "I have an investor wants to buy
The land and all your cows
And will pay you top dollar!"

Sold out
Bought more
Good years
Bad years
I still was building on the dream.

Better bulls
Bigger calves
Improvements made
Bills paid
Still the work just never seemed to end.

Then along came someone else
Who wanted it more than I
So "Sold Out" was the name of the game.
I guess I'm not a Cow Man anymore.

Tumbleweeds (Haiku)

Fly through the dust cloud
Great balls of thorn-laced dead plants
Play Frogger with cars

SCOURED?

Yesterday was one of those
That tries the hearts and very souls
Of those who make their living from the land.

What started as a pleasant breeze
Soon scoured the earth and bent the trees
As though to cleanse the land of human hand.

The tumbleweeds took out wire fences;
Dirt filled the air and dulled the senses
And most cowered safe in sheltering fastness.

But, out upon the wind-blown plains
Cattlemen fought the driven flames
Of wildfires racing 'cross the withered grasses.

Until 'bout Midnight when it lay,
This wind that blew throughout the day,
To give brief respite from it's blasting scour

As though it sought in silent rest
While building strength do its best
Spring cleaning with deep sand-blasted power.

CAMPFIRE COFFEE

Before the light of breaking dawn
I stir the coals of last night's fire
Until the red glow of waking embers
Crackles in the chill.
A little "tinder" care and the licking flames
Seek more substantial fare
Of volatile vapors escaping the dried branches
Tented above.
Soon the fragrances of boiling grounds
Promise warmth to meet the inner needs
As tin cup in hand
I watch the spreading glow
In silence savored.

SPRING WISHES

When the temperature starts to rise
And I wake to clear blue skies;
When the birds begin to sing
It doesn't really mean a thing
Except that Spring is just around the corner.

MUSTANG

The story is told of days long ago
When wild horses ran over the land
From the cold of Alberta to wild Argentina
Roamed many a fleet, wily band.

With blood of the deserts and Andalusia
These hardy wild beasts of the Plain
Descended from stock brought over by ship
To settle the broad Spanish Main

Where some would escape, and others were traded
To natives for food and for hide
To cover in warmth the wandering Spaniards
Across this wild land they did ride.

Over long years, increasing in numbers
They soared 'cross the grasslands with grace
Providing Comanche, Cheyenne and Apache
With mounts of great power o'er this place

They were caught by the lasso or captured in herds
By cowboys and skilled Caballeros.
They were trapped in the canyons and watering places
By Mountain Men and the Llaneros.

They were mounts for the wars that covered the land
And valued for lasting endurance
They carried the soldier in bright uniform
Or warriors with arrows and lance.

THE HAREM

Quality is the name of the game
For purebred cattle herds
So no expense is spared acquiring genes.

They arrive in tanks of nitrogen
In something we call straws
And are delivered in a way that may seem obscene.

It is the most efficient way
For improving the herd quickly
Because the best blood is often far away

So modern technology
Has taken the place
Of the purebred herd bulls today.

However, there are those
Among the lucky few
Who don't face humiliation in a cone

They get to roam the pasture
With the chosen of the crop;
They're like a king who sits upon a throne.

With their harem on display
They stand by the road all day
With an attitude of, "Hey, you – look at me!"

You know it's just their job –
Passing traits on to the mob –
And it's just the way that it was meant to be!

ANOTHER DAY OF WIND

For days on end
The unrelenting wind
Scours the parched land.

The temperatures soar
As the months wear on,
Yet barely mid-Spring.

Removing dead fuel;
Last year's grasses
That might have sustained

The few cattle remaining
On the moistureless land,
Once so verdant.

Tears glisten on a creased face
Whose years of labor
Are loaded on trailers.

Another pasture burns.
Another herd is gone.
Another rancher hunkers down.

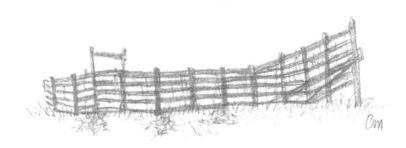

MORE CAMPFIRE COFFEE

The coffee is on and the biscuits are hot
Daylight is burning, get out of your cot.
There's work to be done and it won't do itself
Get up lazy bones or you're gonna be left!

HUNTING ARROWHEADS

Out the back door,
Out through the lot,
I'd head for the pasture
At a slow trot.

Visions of redskins
Danced in my head
As out to the draw
My footsteps had led.

I knew where to hunt;
I'd been there before.
I had one in my pocket
And was looking for more.

Arrowheads!
Arrowheads!
That's all I could think
And fast as a wink
I found one!

I rubbed off the dirt
And then with some spit
I polished it up
And my eyes were all lit

With the sight of this treasure,
This thing I had found,
Just laying right there
On the dry dusty ground.

My mind's eye then saw him
Right there on his horse;
The warrior that lost it
On that water course

So many long years ago.

Prairie Ghost

Standing on the ghostly Plains
He watched as I stopped –
A remnant from the recent past
As through the grass did sigh
A voice mournful, quiet, true,
Of plaintive, chanted prayers
For bloodied spears and meat to eat
And on my head the hairs
Did stand on end as chills swept
O'er my senses there
Of something present in this land
Long passed to ne'er
Return upon the hunt
With rush upon the fleeing herd,
Their lances held on high,
While overhead the bird
Of death circled on the breeze
Awaiting chance to pick the bones
Of those whose path was slow
And destined for the stones
To join them in the sod
So recently trampled under hoof
Where to this day
A sentinel, aloof,
Stands there upon the hill,
A silent Prairie Ghost,
A solitary remnant
Of a vast thundering host.

AROUND AND AROUND

Long summers past and after school
There was a never-ending rule
That I must have a way some funds to earn.

I "chopped" some cotton, stacked some hay
And lots of other things for pay
And even useful skills were there to learn.

But, one I hated way back when
Is even now like it was then,
That's driving a tractor around and around the field.

It was a thing I grew to hate
From early dawn to evening, late
It never to my drifting thoughts appealed.

I just got bored and had a lack
Of staying on the narrow track
Defined by rows laid out so carefully.

My mind would drift 'long other ways,
A tangled and unending maze,
And my mistakes were there for all to see.

So mostly I was sent to plow
The fallow ground as needs allow
In endless circles cutting weeds right down.

And if by chance my mind would drift
The next time 'round my track would shift
To mistakes before they caused a frown.

Those years though long since in the past
Came back just like a sudden blast
Today as I commenced to cut some weeds.

I hooked the shredder on three points
And greased up all the moving joints
Then filled the diesel tank to meet its needs.

The goat weeds and the nettles grew
In many places old and new
Where pasture grasses were what I should see.

And there I started 'round and around
As they succumbed to the chopping sound
And my mind drifted to this memory.

SHORT VS. TALL GRASS

I grew up in a country where the grass was short and strong;
The cows there liked to eat it and it kept them all year long.

Where I live today the grass is usually mighty tall;
It loses all its strength when summer turns to Fall.

And even in the best of times it isn't worth a lot
Although it grows quite well when summer days are long and hot.

The problem is it grows so tall because it's full of water
And it takes a mighty lot of it to feed the bovine daughter.

It's said that you can always take a cow from east to west
But taking them the other way has never worked the best.

The cows back east have larger guts to handle this lush treat,
It gives them the capacity to eat and eat and eat.

But if you ship a cow from west to places way back east
They just can't seem to eat enough to get enough to eat.

BUILDING A FENCE

Take a mark and find the line;
Clear the brush and weeds and vine.

Pound the posts into the ground;
Hope no rocks will there be found.

Set the corners up just right;
String the wires all nice and tight.

Tie the wire with even space;
Then the stays go into place.

A level gate is wanted most
As hinge mounts go into the post.

Hang the gate right in its place;
Wipe the sweat from off your face.

Building fence, the rancher's chore,
Was so much fun, let's build some more!

HEROES WEAR WHITE HATS

My heroes have always been cowboys;
At the top of the list was the King.
He could ride, he could shoot as he whipped the outlaws
And on top of all that he could sing!

He rode on a horse that was everyone's dream
And Trigger was his name;
A gold palomino, swift as could be,
The fastest one in the game.

They don't make 'em like Roy and Dale anymore,
At least not up on the Big Screen.
Today they portray all the cowboys
As ornery, low-down and mean.

Hollywood needs to go back to the day
And make cowboys heroes again.
It's important for roles to be healthy for kids
And help the young boys become men.
(After seeing the saddle and bridle of Roy Rogers in the Briscoe
Museum of Western Art in downtown San Antonio, Texas.)

Visiting the Neighbor

We own a couple of Charolais bulls
That we call Curly and Moe.
Their job is to keep the girls happy
And it's one they seem to know.

Yesterday as I was checking the cows
I looked across the fence
And there was Moe looking at me
Just like he had good sense.

I thought, "No, that can't be him!"
And double-checked the brand
But sure enough it was him alright
As big as a big brass band.

I knew I had to get him back
But the neighbor wasn't home;
Moe wasn't supposed to be in there,
His job was not to roam!

So I opened the gate that's been there for years
Likely put there for just such a case,
And headed afoot 'cross the neighbor's place
Not really wanting a chase.

I figured that Moe was ready to go
Back from whence he came
But no, that wasn't the plan that he had
And so commenced the game

Of me trying to coax him to that tiny gate,
A place where he'd never been,
And just when I'd get him almost to it
He'd circle around me again!

Then he decided to head toward the creek,
And I thought, "Well that's Okay.
He's probably headed to a hole in the fence
That allowed him to come over today."

Of course, I was wrong, as we walked near a mile
With him looking for holes in the fence
Until he got clear to the far south end,
Me following like I had good sense.

Then he turned around and started right back
The way that we had just come,
And I was beginning to wish for some help
And frankly, feeling quite dumb.

He finally made it clear to the gate
I had opened when e'er I did start.
He looked back at me with a smirk on his face
And through it quickly did dart!

I wired it shut so he couldn't get out
And headed him back to his place
With him calling out every few steps or so
As if he had just won a race.

So then my next chore was to go 'round the fence
And figure just how he got out.
I never did find anything out of place
So, I figure he jumped, the big lout.

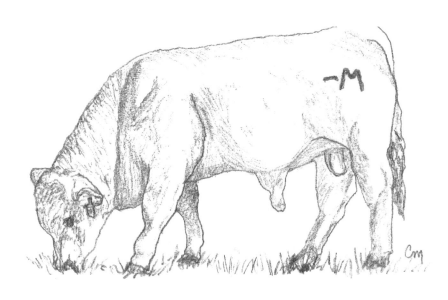

WEANING CALVES

Round them up and sort them out,
The cows go to the right.
Calves all go the other way,
"Watch her, she wants to fight!"

Check your count and don't miss one,
Sometimes the calves slip by,
"Use the gate to cut her off!"
The Boss says with a sigh.

Babies bawling through the fence
To see where Momma stands;
It's not so much they need them,
Fear drives their demands.

It's time for them to grow on up
And make it on their own.
They know how to eat the grass
Just like their Mom has shown

Them since they hit the ground
Several months ago
When they were born into the cold,
And sometimes it would snow.

But life's a cycle going 'round
And this is just a step
Along their earthly journey.
And now they will be kept

In a pen that's set aside
For such a time as this.
And even though she will be close
Their Momma will they miss

For a few days until they have found
That they no longer need
The nourishment that she provides
As they learn to eat their feed.

Very soon they won't depend
On Mom on whom they leaned
And one more time I'll smile and say,
"The calves have all been weaned."

The Passing Storm

It's the middle of July
And I gaze across the range.
From the back of my old cow horse
I sit and watch the weather change.

From a point up on the Caprock
I survey for miles and miles
A parched and dry old grassland
But my face is all in smiles

For boiling to the westward
Are clouds of darkest blue
And a wall of rain approaching
Obscures the range from view.

Then, a cool wind hits me
As the front comes rushing by
And the torrent starts unleashing
From the lightning-streaked sky.

I quickly don my slicker
Against the pouring rain
But I don't mind the drenching
So, I face it with disdain.

Soon the storm is over
And the sun comes shining through
The holes in breaking clouds
On a land brand spanking new

And I hear the birds singing
In the brush along the cliff
And their song sets my smile wider
As it gives my heart a lift.

I hear the cows bawling
Searching out their calves again
Or, maybe they're just voicing
Their thanks for all the rain.

And I take off my hat
To give thanks for such a scene
And would swear that as I'm watching
The grass is turning green.

Stock Market Wisdom

Making sense of the stock market
Is a challenge to most of us.
It seems the boys on Wall Street
Are constantly stirring up a fuss
Whenever they want to see a stock move.
The sad thing is we are all looking for a win
So we put our money down
Although our chance is thin.
And we listen to the mavens
From the big stock brokerage firms
Tell us where to put our dollars
That we've worked so hard to earn.
Just like a flock of sheep
We go rushing where they say,
Hoping we will make a killing
On the stock market today.
But Wall Street just keeps laughing
As we put our savings down
'Cause they went short as we went long
And the profit went to town.
I wish I'd listened to the rancher
Whose wisdom now makes sense;
Keep your money in the bank
And your stock behind a fence.

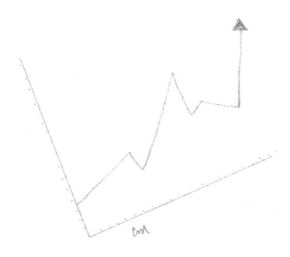

TUMBLEWEED

Tumbling, tumbling –
Incessantly rolling 'cross the prairie.
Gathering cotton lint
And bits of paper,
The tumbleweed
Visits the neighbor
But can't seem to cross the fence
Until a sudden gust
Lifts it high
And it flies through the air.
It soars,
It bounces,
It rolls on and on
Until it lodges
With its buddies in the corner
By the barn
Where the field mice
Will have a field day
Tonight.

RAIN

I love to hear the rain.
It is like a thin sheet of tin rattling
As it peppers the windows,
The skylights,
The sidewalk.
The low sound of thunder
(The "potato wagon turning over"
Of my youth) brings a promise
Of violence,
Of renewal,
Or both,
As it slowly grows closer.
It is spring.
Officially.
In reality.
As the trees bloom
And the leaves unfold
And I sneeze
From the whiff of pollen on the air.

ON THE HORIZON A PUFF OF WHITE

On the horizon a puff of cloud
Appears to grow from nothing.
Its fluffy whiteness slowly deepens
To a grayish blue as it pulls
The moisture into
Its blossom.

Suddenly, a slender bolt
Dashes to the ground
And the low
Vibration
Rolls across the prairie until
The panes in the windows
Lightly rattle.

A gentle breeze begins to stir
The grass and bend it
Lightly toward the
Approaching
Cloud.

It is growing higher and wider
And imperceptibly a
Dim curtain
Appears
Below.

It is the rain beginning to reach
From the expanding mass
That blots the sky
In the
West.

The grays turn to blues with an
Occasional streak of white
That takes on a greenish
Tint as the storm
Swells across
The sky

Until it stretches across the horizon
And the wispy edges begin
To pass overhead
And blot the
Last rays
Of Sun.

The wind is now gusting and changing
Directions continually until
It suddenly ceases
In eerie silence
And the low
Warble of
Sirens

I hear in the distance warning all
To take shelter because
A possible tornado
Has been sighted
Somewhere
Within.

And the hail begins to fall at intervals
Until a low roar like an approaching
Train begins to grow louder
And louder as though
The train is coming
Right at me and
I know that it
Is time to run
Into the house
And into the
Basement
And wait
Until it
Passes
On,
On,
On,
On....

PEACEFUL LABORS

Planting, sowing,
Raking, hoeing,
Weeding, mowing,
Trimming, growing.
Water hoses,
Grass and roses,
Butterflies and bees,
Large shade trees.
Peace sublime;
It's springtime.

UNCOMMON

This morning was beautiful as I rose early to a temperature around 50
degrees. There was light rain during the night and the air is clear,
cool and moist. The pastures are green with flowers peeking
everywhere; the wheat is heavy with grain before the ripening;
the corn is quickly growing and there are cattle ankle-deep
in grass almost everywhere I turn. This to me is
the most beautiful time of year
in the Texas Panhandle.

The morning mists
Are darkened shadows
Hanging in the dips
And valleys of the Plains
Which stretch onward
For miles in all directions
From my vantage on
The high flat ground.
The meadowlark's
Twee-phut-weee trills
In the otherwise silent
Coolness of the day
Before the common stirring
Begins.

MISTY SERENITY

The early morning mist
Rising over the coolness
Evokes a serenity of place
That contradicts
The activity of the day.
Muffled sounds punctuate
The stillness yet are unable
To displace the peacefulness.
A perfect start to the week.

SUNSETS

Sunset on the open plains
Is a sight to behold.
The sky is filled with blues,
Yellows, reds and gold.

Bold strokes paint the
Flame of day
To slowly fade
Across the way

'Til only memories
Of the vivid hues
Are left upon the
Minds-eye view.

INTO THE FURNACE

A hot dry wind
Blows across the Plains
Sucking the lifeblood of the prairie
In its searing blast.

The succulence
Of the rain engorged leaves
Is gone and the withered remains
Curl into grayish husks

Of their former selves.
Yet on the horizon
Tower the billowing
Marshmallow shapes of

Cumulus clouds reaching through
The heat blasted hole into the
Cooler air above
Where the hailstones form.

Relief comes at a price.

MOUNTAINS AND HISTORY

Raton Pass,
Trinidad,
Coal mines,
Purgatorie River,
Bosque de Oso,
Oil wells,
Stonewall,
Monument Lake,
Cucharras Pass,
Cordova Pass,
Spanish Peaks,
Adobe,
Santa Fe Trail,
Kit Carson,
Charles Bent,
Lucien Maxwell,
Doc Holiday,
Bat Masterson,
Wyatt Earp,
Matador Ranch,
Prairie Land and Cattle,
Mexican Food,
Vermejo Park,
Elk.
The things of this day.

PRAIRIE OASIS

Shadows flicker on the ground
Beside the cool water
Trickling from a concrete tank
To which life is drawn.

The rhythmic mechanical clanking
Of sucker rod
Drawing the clear liquid
From beneath the earth is a welcome sound.

Hand cupped to the pipe
To catch the icy elixir
The old cowboy splashes
Dust from his face

As Traveler slurps noisily
From the tank beside him.
Tracks of quail and coyote
And other denizens

Of the dry plains rim the pool
Where the overflow
Purposefully sustains
The creatures in need.

The Rising and the Setting Eclipsed

This morning as I drove to work
I watched the setting moon
Eclipsed by earth's shadow
As it sank into the horizon

While in my rear-view mirror
I at the same time saw
The glowing ball of orange sun
Rising out of the horizon

I was struck with wonder
At the beauty of the morning
While filled with thoughts
Of primitive man delving

Into the mystery that
Could only leave them wondering
If their world was ending
Only to be born again.

SEARCH FOR WORDS

As the pre-dawn light
Rose behind me
I watched the pearlescent orb
Slowly evolve into a buttery
Disk blushing with rising pinkness
That intensified to red
And then magenta
As it met the mists
Of the horizon
Where it sank
Into the blue violet haze
Only to emerge briefly
As a faded grayish ghost of light
Before being eaten
By the earth itself.
So went my morning commute.

WINTER NIGHT SKY

Cold and clear
I walk into the night
Thinking hurry
To the task
For it is cold
And I prefer the warmth inside
When suddenly
The quietness,

The blackness,

The brilliance,

Of stars twinkling
Overhead
Captures me
And stillness

Replaces hurry
With the realization
That I miss the show
While snug within my cave.
It is only when I venture into the cold
That I experience
This gift.

AND IT SNOWS

The cold wind blows
And it snows

So that drifts form
As the storm

Scours the field
And I shield

My stinging face
In this place

Where the bitter cold
Seems to enfold

While I desire
A roaring fire

Where I may warm
This frozen form

As the cold wind blows
And it snows.

The Wind Blows

Restlessly
Incessantly
Relentlessly
The wind blows

The air is filled
With the tiny grains
That should be held
By growing things

Instead
The wind blows
The sand moves
The tiny stalks with newborn leaves
Shrivel beneath the onslaught

No
Not the Dust Bowl
Just spring
In the southern reaches
Of the Great Plains.

August Storms

The golden grasses
Crackle under foot
As dusty odors
Rise from my passing.

Even the insects
Are silently waiting
As the tiny dot of promise
Builds on the horizon.

A gentle breeze stirs
The drooping leaves
Of plants not native
To the arid clime.

Hope springs
In the blossoming white puffs
That appear mysteriously
In the blueness of the sky.

Gathering,
The whiteness turns gray
And then the deepest blue
As it hangs curtains on the horizon.

The breeze strengthens
And even the hard stems
Of golden grasses
Begin to shiver with excitement.

As the curtain approaches
A brown smudge appears
Rising against the darkness,
Swelling to a rolling wall.

The odor of dust
Permeates the rising wind
And the first stinging particles
Assail upturned faces

As dollops of moisture
Splash muddy blotches
On greedy surfaces
That quickly absorb.

Brown gives way
To greens and whites
On the backdrop
Of deepest blue-black.

Whack!
Whack, whack!
Pingggggg!
Run!

Peas and marbles
Golf balls and baseballs,
The roar grows
And overwhelms.

The horizon moves nearer
As objects fade
Beneath the torrent
Rolling across the plains.

Prayers answered.
More prayers said.
Fear and thanksgiving
Together swell.

Renewal
Comes
With
Trial.

RAINBOWS

Stealthy footsteps on damp pine needles
Fall…silently
Against the constant murmur, gurgle, singing
Water burbling
Growing louder yet never changing
Deceptively deep
River rushing over pebbles
Rocks
Boulders
Snags with eddying pools of calm no longer clear
Holes
Where lightly placed temptation
Teases
Seeking silver flashes and splashes
Tugging
Struggling
Dashing
Diving
Striving
Carefully netted morsel
Gently released
To grow for next time.

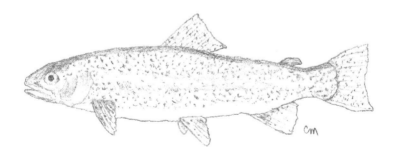

THE WIND BLEW TODAY

The wind blew today.
Tumbleweeds
Piled high against the fences.
The gritty blast
Transformed the sunset
Into a hazy glow
That is quickly
Fading.

RED BREMMER

Way deep in East Texas where swamp gases rise
And sweat from your head runs into your eyes,
The ranchers all have a strange kind of beast
That can handle the pests and the oppressive heat.

They're made with lots of extra leather
That helps them to live in that miserable weather.
Their ears are quite long and hang by their head;
They range in colors across gray, black and red.

Most are quite gentle though few think it so
Because of bulls seen in the big rodeo
Who pitch off the bean trying to cling to their back
Until he goes flying to the ground with a whack.

With ancestors who hailed from far Bangalore
Halfway 'cross the world they've come to our shore
To live in the swamps through the heat of the summers
These strange long-eared critters the folks there call Bremmers.

Sometimes a Sunrise

Sometimes a sunrise
Will light up the sky
As though the world were on fire.

Sometimes it bursts
With rays of the dawn
Leaping out from the dark horizon.

Sometimes a sunrise
Presages a storm;
Vermillion splashed on the clouds.

Sometimes a sunrise
Is just in my eye
And I can't really see where I'm going....

Some Days the Wind

A faint odor of dust lingers on the air
As I sit inside and work from my chair.
Around me drones the incessant roar
Of the howling wind outside my door.

It is days like this I wonder why
I live in this place windswept and dry
Where the sky can turn an ugly brown
From dirt that is blowing round and around

And driving the road is like a video game
Where tumbleweeds roll down the middle of same
Where fields try to move one grain at a time
Or, sometimes as rocks as big as a dime.

Yep, it's times like these that I'd like to go
To a place where it's green and the wind doesn't blow,
Where trees touch the sky and bright waters flow
And cattle graze in the valley below

But then I remember the wind too shall pass
And the beautiful sky no place can surpass
With air that's so pure you can see for days
As I dream in the warmth of gentle sun rays;

Where humidity is never too high or too low
And the quiet gentle breezes always blow
Across the endless sea of grass
Where once the scouring wind did pass.

Food and Energy

The whirling blades turn
Restlessly

The cattle graze
Quietly

The horizon stretches
Endlessly

Energy flows
Food grows

SPRING'S BLESSED CURSES

Springtime is the time of year
When the earth is clothed anew
In a colorful arrangement
Topped off with skies so blue.

The birds begin to sing again
And trees burst forth in leaf,
Flowers spring from within the earth
With colors beyond belief.

The cool breeze blowing across the land
Spreads pollen far and near,
Creating life in blooming plants
And fruit to bring us cheer.

But springtime brings us other things
Like floods and hail and such,
That we who live upon the earth
Don't care for all that much.

And that pollen, bringing life anew,
Creates for some of us
A runny nose and itching eyes
That make us want to cuss.

And growing things create work,
To prevent spreading out of hand,
Like mowing yards and trimming trees
And hoeing weeds upon the land.

And in the home there is no rest
For cleaning there must be
In closets and places you would think
Should be completely dust free.

It is a blessing, yes indeed,
This springing forth anew;
But with the blessing comes the curse
Of a million things to do!

A HINT OF MOISTURE

There was the smell of rain
On the air last night
And a touch of cooler weather

The promised moisture
Only came near
But left us dry as ever

And today again
The wind does blow,
The sun is bright as ever

But finally now
We've had a glimpse
Of perhaps some better weather.

WET LEAVES

Wet leaves
They stick to your feet
And follow you in
Where they aren't supposed to be

Wet leaves
They cling to your hair
Then fall to the floor
Leaving mess everywhere

Wet leaves
They stick to your clothes
When you brush them all off
They might stick to your nose

Wet leaves
They lay on the ground
And when you walk o'er
It makes nary a sound

Wet leaves
They are wet from the rain
As it soaks into the ground
Where the waters all drain

Wet leaves
They cover the earth
Making food for the worms
Until Spring's new birth

THE SCENT OF RAIN

Once again the rains have passed us by. Each day for the last several,
the National Weather Service has shown us to have a significant
chance of rain. Heavy showers have fallen in many places around us,
but we received only one tenth of an inch. It is dry.

First a hint of puffy white
Appears up in the sky
Then slowly grows and grows and grows
Until it fills the eye.

The promise of the quenching drops
Wafts across the land
On gentle breezes flowing by
This parched and weary strand.

The leaden gray with streaks of light
Approaches from the west
With winds that cool the sultry land
And promise moist rest.

The sand that stings blows ever higher,
The cattle turn their back,
The storm clouds flow across the land,
The sky turns nearly black.

But soon it passes on its way,
It's promise hoped in vain,
Leaving nothing here behind
Except a scent of rain.

THE GENTLE SOUND OF RAIN

This morning I awoke
To the quiet sound of rain
Upon this dry and dusty arid plain

It brought a gentle comfort
As I lay there in my bed
Thinking how it brought a peace into my head

I thought how only yesterday
The dust arose like smoke
And clogged the air I breathed and made me almost choke

And I remembered cattle coughing
Standing still beneath the shade
The few scraggly trees and bushes made

But the simple sound of moisture
Falling gently from the sky
Promised their relief was surely nigh

In my head I thanked my Maker
For the blessings He bestows
Then quietly rose and slipped into my clothes

And walked to the window
To look out upon the rain
Falling ever gently on this sun-scorched weary plain

A METEOR

Flitting there across my sight
A flash lit up the starry night,
An omen, some would say in days of old.

As I watched there in wonder
My thoughts began to ponder
How it had traveled across the spaces cold

To die in flash of streaking light
And bring to gazing eyes delight
With wishes breathed by those who were below

This ancient wonder in the sky
Snuffed out before my very eye
From distant places I will never know.

THE HAWK

From his perch upon a post
The silent watcher spies
Movement in the sheltering grass
Wherein a creature lies

In wait for chance to find a seed
To make a scanty meal
Or, loosened stems with which to line
Her nest where she would seal

The pink and hairless squirming babes
Who wait her quiet return
That they might suckle at her breast
Until large enough to learn

Their way out in the larger world
That waits just on the verge
Beyond the tangle where they live
Where they will soon emerge.

But then a silent plunge begins
With speed beyond belief
Into the grass with talons spread
That leaves the babes in grief

For mother who will ne'er return
To the soon silent nest.
Her life once lived so furtively
Now lies ever in rest.

WINGED AND DANGEROUS

Summer is a time of year
With many creatures, small and dear,
That disappear when winter's chills abound.

Among them is a tiny thing
Which can seem vicious, oh, so mean,
Near any pool of moisture on the ground.

It has a long and narrow probe
For piercing skin wherever it goes
To drink from living rivers there beneath.

And when I can, I swat the thing
Which leaves a splash of red on me
And often words, unkind, escape my teeth.

For though she's small and merely seeks
Something there which she might eat
I begrudge her every single liquid bite.

So, if I see her land on me
I swat her, quick, before she can flee
And watch for all her friends that try to light.

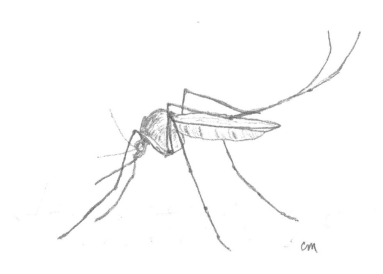

A Remembered Opening Day

Hunting season comes around
In Fall of every year;
Through much of this great country
The quest is for the deer.

But I grew up on the Plains
Where deer were scarce to see;
It was hunting for the birds
That held excitement for me.

First came dove, how swift they flew
Across the bright blue skies;
To get the hang of hunting them
Took many, many tries.

I think of when the first I shot,
I was well short of ten,
But I felt that I was mighty tall
To go hunting with the men.

I don't recall who all was there
But it was at the ranch;
Dad was far the better shot
Upon the family branch.

But Grandpa was the one who set me
In the pumphouse door
To watch out toward the water tank
For one, or maybe more

Of those swift creatures who might
Light upon the fence.
That gave me an advantage
When my shot occurred and hence

I didn't try to take them
As they darted through the air;
No one then had told me
That it wasn't really fair.

So, I set there on a bucket
With Mom's .410 in hand
And waited for the dull gray birds
Upon the fence to land.

And when one finally did
I carefully lined my shot
And pulled the small black trigger
While pointing at the spot.

And the blast sent me a flying
Off the bucket to the ground
And dazed, I went to looking
If the target I had found.

And sure enough I got him
Though I was somewhat bruised.
Then I dusted off my britches
And ejected the shell that I had used.

I leaned my mighty weapon
Up against the pumphouse wall
And proceeded to the place
Where my quarry had to fall.

As I showed it to my Grandpa
Who was grinning ear to ear
I had to say I wasn't expecting
To get knocked upon my rear.

COYOTE

Far across the pasture upon a slight rise
I see you watching me,
Knowing that you saw
My approach long before I was aware
Of your presence.

You drop your head and tail and begin
To trot at a measured pace
In the general direction
Of a copse of trees
Across the fence.

Were you hunting and I interrupted
Or, were you headed home
From an all-night chase
With your buddies
And their yipping chorus?

There is abundance now, but it was
A lean summer in which the
Fare was scarce and difficult
Yet, you look to be
Well nourished.

You are part of the balance that I know
Is necessary yet,
I am unforgiving when I see you
In springtime around the
Newborn calves.

Right now I am tolerant of your presence
But beware come spring,
For I will be watching and
If you stray too close I might
Send a shot your way.

DAYDREAMING

In my office there's no window to look out upon the world
So, I must use the window in my mind
To allow my drifting consciousness to wander where it will
And see what new adventures it might find.

Instead of looking out upon a street filled with cars
Or, a parking lot, or even yards of grass,
My thoughts drift to the mountains and a cold tumbling stream
Or, to a deep cold lake as still as glass

With surface broken only by the tiny lure
I would toss out as temptation for a fish
Until I feel the tug, almost like electric shock,
Of a glistening rainbow trout as I would wish.

There upon the distant shore I see across the way,
A regal elk come stepping from the wood
To drink from crystal waters where I seek tricky prey.
Then he looks upon the place whereon I stood

And I salute him for his boldness, for his total lack of fear,
As he sounds his eerie cry into the air
That calls his tiny harem down to drink there by his side
While he keeps a silent watch upon them there.

A fog comes slowly drifting down the wooded mountainside
To obscure the vision far across the lake
And again, I see the ripples from the fish that I have sought
With temptation for the bait I hoped he'd take

Until the whole scene finally faded from my mind
Into a blank computer screen before
I realized what happened as I sought to fill the page,
Preferring to be daydreaming once more....

A Red-Tailed Hawk

Soaring o'er the windy plain
He surveys his vast domain
Searching out a morsel for his meal.

A flash of color on his tail
As he continues high to sail
On currents only he can feel.

He swoops lower on his course
Toward some small denizen's remorse
That sought to grab a seed or, maybe two.

On silent wings he does not stray
As lower still he's on his way,
Unerring aim, he pounces straight and true.

Then rising once again we see
The bite his talons could not flee,
The mighty wings soon rise above the stalk

Where one small mouse has met his end
With no way that he could defend
Against the striking of the Red-tailed hawk.

TIES THAT BIND

In between the earth and space
There stands an organism
That ties the two together.

With arms that stretch toward the sky
It seeks the sun's vast energy
And scours the air for molecules

While sending deep into the earth
Its toes to drink the moisture there
And mine for needed minerals.

Upon its limbs in summer garb
Are tiny engines made to capture
Light that falls upon them.

That light excites the cells to bind
The carbon waste of others
And free the oxygen of life

To be breathed by those who need
This catalyst for their vital function.
It stores the carbon in itself

In fibrous growth that helps it stand
Against the storms and winds
And ravages that assail

To give it strength which makes
It valued by the builder for
Shelter and other usefulness.

It breaks the earth with its strong feet
Allowing microbes to enter there
And further free the needed wealth

Of minerals contained therein
Which enrich the lives of smaller plants
That need such nutrition

To then be used by beings
Higher still to fulfill the cycle
Until, decomposed, they fill the earth again.

A tree
Is key.

THE HIGH PLAINS

Pale straws bend as unseen
Forces sweep
Across the nearly featureless
Landscape
That stretches for miles
Unending.
Broken occasionally by
Deep green
Sprays of needles and
Dried stalk
Of the spiny growth
Of Yucca.

I lean slightly into
The invisible
Never-ending force of
The wind,
That restless, timeless
Bringer
Of storms and drought
And change
Upon this landscape
Swept flat
By Eons of scouring
Movement.

I am covered by a sense of
Peace
When a slight hint of dust
Tickles
My nostrils as I gaze
Across
The seemingly forever
Plains.
It is the serenity of being
Home.

FALL WEATHER

Light slowly seeps into awareness
As the dim outline of trees in the distance
Materialize above the silvery fog
Which hangs along the creek.

The cool dampness is a pleasant change
From the sultry heat which has hung on
Long past the peak of summer
When it is expected.

The cattle move like specters through the mist
As they harvest the wet succulence of the recent growth
From rains which seemed long delayed
As the heat of August domed the land.

A sense that Fall has arrived has finally
Leaped from the start of school and
The Friday night rituals of football and marching band
To the weather itself.

The harvest is in full swing as crops
Are brought into the storehouse against the needs
Of the looming months of cold
And rest for the land

As it hibernates until the time when earthly tilt
Brings longer days again which are
Warmed by the nearer sun which releases
Dormant seeds to spring anew.

ALTERNATIVE ENERGY

Towering above the mesa
The row of white needles
Punctures the blue with
Rotating scythes that
Capture the power of
The wind. Lined for miles
Across the prairie they
Are seen for great distances
And yet stretch over
Such an area that
They can't all be seen at once.
The wind blows,
The blades turn,
Slowly spinning the
Turbines that generate
Electricity to flow
Into the grid.

THE LAND OF PROMISE

The children are crying from the hunger
That has plagued his family for generations
Because the meager sustenance purchased
By a hard day's labor barely keeps them alive.
At five feet, two inches, Jose is the tallest
In his family of nine surviving siblings.
His heart is full of fear because the only
Way to improve his family's lot is to travel
North across six hundred miles of desert
To where the opportunity for a difference begins.

Across the river is a patrol that seems ever vigilant.
Yet the stories abound that there are many ways
To enter the Land of Promise. The small sack
That carries all his possessions is no hindrance,
But also, no help, because none in his family
Have ever managed to save enough to pay the
Fees that the "coyotes," the human smugglers,
Demand for safe passage. So, it must be the river.

Lost in a wilderness of thorns, he wanders,
Searching for water that his body needs
To replenish the reserves which are almost depleted.
He stumbles across a stock tank that,
Although stagnant and warm, provides
That which is necessary for survival. He hears,
In the distance, the sound of a motor approaching
And knows that he must hide if he is to
Reach his cousin that is supposed to be
Living somewhere in San Antonio.

After weeks of travel, mostly on foot,
He knocks timidly at the door of Fernando,
His mother's cousin. Reluctantly he is allowed
To enter where he is fed and through family news,
Eventually accepted as someone to be trusted.

If only he could find some job that would
Give him the means to live and to send money
Back to his family, he would be happy.
He is told there are no jobs to be had here
But there is work in the feedlots far to the north.

"Ernesto drives a truck hauling produce from the
Valley to Lubbock and he will take you, but
You must be careful to do everything that he says
Because the Patrol has been watching Ernesto.
If they catch you, they will send you back.
You must stay beneath the tarp, Jose, if you
Want to make it safely. You will be on your
Own to get from Lubbock to Hereford, but
Once you are there, find Emilio, he will help you."

"Can you drive? Can you use a rope? Do you
Know how to doctor cattle? Do you speak any
English? Do you have warm clothes? I will
Get you a Social Security card and a driver's license
To use, but you must remember, your name is
John. You will bring your check to me when
You are paid and I will keep part for the rent
You will owe me, part for your food, and part
To pay for the card and the license. You will
Shovel the feed bunks and clean the tanks
And anything else that they ask you to do."

Six months later, Jose/John can speak enough
English to get around without much help. He
Lives with three others in a room behind the
Laundromat where they cook on a single hotplate.
He has sent twelve hundred dollars to his family
That he misses very much. It is a fortune to them.
In this Land of Promise the work is hard.
He yearns
For the day that he can return to his home
And start his own business and a family.

OTHER THOUGHTS

THE BOSSES ARE MANY

It has been a while since I quit my job
That was not what it was billed to be
And now I'm out here on my own
Supposedly working just for me.
But, here in the ranks of the self-employed
Is not for the weak of heart;
It's a place where the toils of the daily grind
Are from sunup to well after dark.
It matters not what you might do,
As you put in countless hours
On services or something to sell –
Whatever is in your powers.
Whether artist, mechanic or singer of song
In the end it's for a bright shiny penny
That will pay for the groceries, or maybe the rent
So, instead of one boss now there's many!

QUESTIONS AND ANSWERS

To question, to ponder, to think far ahead
Is something that's rarely encountered.
Most people think to the end of their nose
And rarely go very much farther.

They need guidance, direction and sometimes a shove
To get them to take a step forward.
They can't help it because it's the way they were trained
From grade school and onward through college.

We are taught to be parts in a great big machine
To conform and act much like each other
So if one part is broken another fits in
And the ponderous steps are unaltered.

What to do with a thinker who doesn't fit in
Is a question the "Masters" might answer
Just leave them behind, they are worthless to us
And so genius is often abandoned.

But, every so often one overcomes pain
To take others a giant step forward.
Despite the battle against those who're entrenched
In controlling positions of power.

Be the thinker, disrupter, who doesn't fit in
Make your mark in the world by your wit.
Take on the headwinds or, swim up the stream
Change this world for its own betterment.

MAKING DECISIONS

Fear is oft the driving force
That blankets many mind
When faced with a decision.

It's fear of being in the wrong.

This failure often means inaction
Though time is of the essence
In this fast-paced world we're in.

Choose now – don't wait too long

Or the opportunity will pass you by
While you weigh all the options
And bounce your thoughts off others.

It is simply a decision -- a choice of direction.

Decisions may be right or may be wrong
It often doesn't matter
It's just the first step on a pathway.

But, what if it's the wrong one?

Then simply make another decision.

INSPIRATION

Inspiration is a fickle thing,
It comes and then it goes.
Sometimes it feels like poetry,
At others, simple prose.

From whence it comes I often wonder,
Is it something in the air
Or, is it something from our Maker
To the people in His care?

Sometimes it strikes out of the blue
Like lightening from a cloud,
And other times it sneaks in quiet
While supplicating, bowed.

It seems to strike while in the shower
Or, waking from deep sleep
When the mind is freed to wander
Filing thoughts we wish to keep.

It's critical for artists
Musicians and all such
Who depend on creative genius
And the Muse's subtle touch.

Where it's needed is in business
As we go about our day
Where we can make a lasting difference
Through what we do and what we say.

So, listen for the quiet voice
As it whispers in your ear.
Be inspired to make a difference
To others far and near.

SEIZE THE MOMENT

In the glass of time to each of us allotted,
The grains slip silently downward,
Accumulating in a cone of memories
That represents the things which have shaped us.
Yet, there above in the upper chamber
Are many more grains that have not fallen
Which represent what lies before us.
Constricted through each passing moment,
These tiny silicate crystals flow unceasingly.
As that not yet transpired diminishes
In the brief passage of experience
We must seize each grain with fervor.

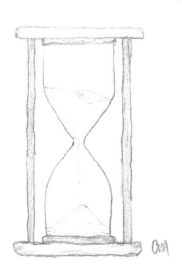

Is it Wisdom?

Some of us get wise.
Some just get old.
They say that fortune favors the bold.

Some of us are bold.
Others are not.
Fortune just means of money you have made a lot.

So, is it just the money?
Or, is it something more
That drives you to get up, get dressed and head right out the door?

Why do you do what you do?

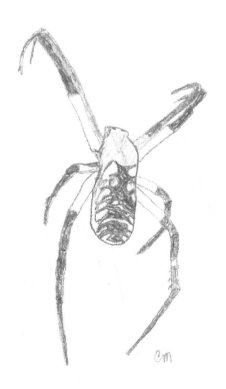

Trying to Think

It seems that on those days when I struggle with my thoughts
The distractions mount to a level quite unbearable.
They grate upon my nerves until I want to burst
And let my temper get the very best of me.

It is then that I must pause and appeal unto my Maker
For patience that will quench the kindled fire
Of anger that is swelling up inside
Before it grows so strong that it breaks free.

So, I pause and seek that quiet place that hides down in my soul
Where Peace abounds despite surrounding flames
And I am able once again to tamp the fires within,
That raging storm that others rarely see.

FULL MOON

A single pearl
Upon a thread that fades
Into the blackness
Broken with sparkling
Sequins of light
Pulls upon the waters
And the emotions.
Laughter is louder,
Moods are darker,
Desires are sharper,
Eyes are brighter,
And strange deeds
Are done.
Let the wolf howl!

ONE MAN'S TREASURE...

The sign said,
"Going out of business sale,"
So we stopped
Because we like antiques
And that was what the other sign said.
In a former use it was
A boarding house
But now it contained
Leftovers from estate sales,
Yard sales,
Any kind of sales that
Had items long past their prime
That might be considered collectibles
Or maybe vintage
And rarely antique.
The memories rose from the
Stacks and shelves and piles
Like ghosts of the former boarders
That once occupied the 23 rooms
While they sought a living
In the oil boom town
Long deflated.
It was a pleasant hour of
Strolling and looking
And laughing and
Figuring out what the use might have been
Of some strange utensil.
The books always intrigue
But they were well picked over
And nothing caught my eye
That didn't already occupy
A place at home.
It was interesting looking at
The items that
To the former owners
Were treasures I'm sure
But to me were just Junk

SHOPPING, NOT BUYING

Shopping wears me out.
Now don't get me wrong,
I can buy with the best of 'em.
It's the shopping that's hard.
You look and you look
And then drive someplace else
And you look and you look
And still no decision is made.
Things that I would reject
In less than a heartbeat
Get looked at and talked about
And critiqued and discussed
Until I'm thinking, "let's move on,
We already know this isn't it!"
Yet, we keep looking and shopping –
Not buying at all. It makes me tired
And I struggle to maintain
A good attitude about the process
That is involved in deciding.
Me – I like to make a quick tour
And assemble ideas for later processing at home,
Or while doing something else.
I can make up my mind a lot better
Without continuing to add to the clutter
By looking and looking and looking
And looking and looking and –
I think you get the message.
Shopping is not my thing.
It makes me tired.
I get grouchy.
Narrow it down for me.
I'm a buyer, not a shopper
Is that a male thing?

HAMBURGER AND FRIES

I like hamburgers.
They may not be health food,
But I like them.
I prefer them to be made
In the least healthy way;
I like them fried.
Fried on a griddle
And fry the bun too;
Just a little bit toasty
And a little bit greasy.
I like my burgers
With a touch of California
By adding avocado
Or, I like them
New Mexico style
With grilled green Chile peppers.
Or I like them Texas style
With jalapenos on them.
I like hamburgers.
I prefer bread-and-butter pickles
Instead of the dill.
I don't care for onion
Or lettuce but
I do like tomato –
Big, juicy slices of tomato
Fresh from the garden
That cover the meat
Completely.
My burgers don't have to be fried,
I'll take them cooked on the grill outdoors
Or from under the broiler
With Tabasco Sauce
And seasoned salt
To spice them up a little.
I like hamburgers.
And while you're at it
I'll take a side of fries.

STRAW HAT WEATHER

Sun broiling,
Umbrellas shading,
Mowers
Mowing,
Everything growing,
Roses blooming.

Iced tea
Sipping,

Heat blistering,
Everyone
Roasting –
Even me!

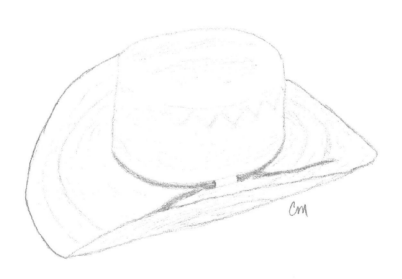

Workout

I am constantly amused
By those who are confused
About simple things in life.

They buy a membership to the gym
To stay fit and trim
To look good for their husband or wife.

Then they head into town
To take a look around
For some labor saving device

That will make pulling weeds
A task of quiet ease
And not even think twice.

Then a mower for riding
Not a push one for striding
Around and around their lawn

Is the next acquisition
For their lofty position
Won't let them do work like a pawn.

Why work up a sweat
When you wash the Corvette?
Hire a college kid needing some bread.

Don't paint your own house
Pay a friend of your spouse
To apply it evenly spread.

And all of those jobs
That need labor in gobs
Are beneath the dignity

So have them all done
By somebody's son
Then you won't have to get dirty.

If work is so bad
That you hire some young lad
To labor out there in the yard

Why is it you spend
Most days and weekend
In the gym working so hard?

THE RETURN

Vacations
Are a time
Where we spend
Days getting our minds
Off of work
Only to find
That when we finally
Forget about work
It's time to go back.

Vacations
Are a time
Where we spend
A lot of energy having fun
Only to find
We must return to work
To recover
From all the effort
We put into relaxing.

Vacations
Are a time
Where we leave
The work to be done
By others
Only to find
That it piled up
While we were gone
And awaits our return.

AGING

Activism
Turn to apathy
And then remembrance.

A cause
Becomes a lost cause
Until it is an "if only."

Restless energy
Replaced by patient endurance
Rests in tales of past exploits.

Dreams
Fade into reality
Merging to memories.

Youth
Grows to middle-age
And finally the wisdom of the elderly.

Daylight Savings Swing Time

Each Spring with Daylight Savings time
We set our clocks ahead
Then gripe and moan of that lost hour
Of sleep we missed in bed.

We wish to leave well enough alone
And forego the seasonal fix
Until we readjust internal clocks
To 5 o'clock being six!

Once again the sun is rising
As to work we drive.
And though for a day or two it's hard
We know that we'll survive

Especially as the days grow warm
And we see the blooming of the spring.
Then we dig out that bag of clubs
And get back in the swing!

OPTIMIST OR PESSIMIST

There is an old saying
That you can tell the difference
Between an optimist
And a pessimist
By how they view the cup.

One sees only what is gone
And thinks that he is doomed
Because his share –
That which remains –
Cannot possibly be enough.

The other has a different view
And sees what lies therein
With the thought that he is blessed
To have something
In his cup from which to drink.

Me, I'm more of a realist
When I view the cup half-full
I see what coffee there remains
And wonder,
Should I drink it cold or put it in the microwave?

VEGETATING

Best of intentions
Don't get it done
Whatever IT happens to be.

I put it off
And make excuses
If it's not important to me.

Like those minor repairs
That seem to pop up
Every week or so

Or those projects I think
Would be really worthwhile
That I just seem to let go.

It makes me wonder
Why Saturday morn
Motivation seems to evaporate

While I just sit back
And accomplish nothing
Except perhaps, vegetate.

ROUGH TRANSITION

Spring sprung,
But winter hasn't given up yet.
Blossoms bloomed,
The freeze tonight will turn them brown.

Dust rises
As southern winds bring warmth.
Tumbleweeds roll
As northern winds bring cold.

Seasons change
But none transition smoothly.
People age;
Few can do so gracefully.

SHAKEN AND STIRRED

In my dream
I was alone in a crowd,
Laughed at and scorned.

In my dream
The building shook –
It rolled down the hill.

I stood looking up
And told of my ride;
I was not believed.

I walked away
Dazed,
Confused.

Was it just a dream?

RESTLESS

Sometimes out there beyond my reach
Is something that escapes me.
It causes me to walk the floor
Wondering what I don't see.

It's like there's something I should do
But don't know what it might be
And so, I go from here to there
Looking for the right key

To unlock the thing that's out there –
Maybe something I should do
And I would do it gladly –
This thing that really bugs me.

Instead, I get so restless
Thinking I am missing something
That I bounce from here to yonder
And annoy those around me

While I never stop the searching
For this thing that I can't figure
That causes such disquiet
Way down deep inside me.

SWEAT AND BURN

I guess I'm getting older,
Things don't work like they used to.
So, I got a little program
That shows me what to do.

I play it on the t.v.
And this guy is jumping 'round
Doing all these calisthenics
To a really upbeat sound.

It's supposed to make me better,
Get my heart in shape and all,
But after a few minutes
I'm down to just a crawl.

My muscles just don't work like that –
The way that they're supposed to
So, I only do them part of the way
Like the guy says I should do.

But after thirty minutes
He hasn't broken a sweat
While I'm dripping a big puddle
There on my workout mat.

I huff and puff around the floor
While he durn near sings a song
And bounces all around the place
Bringing everyone along.

I wonder if it's worth it,
This working up a sweat,
In time I should get better
But I'm not about to bet.

Just how I got in this bad shape
Keeps pressing on my mind.
It must be all those tasty foods
That to me have been unkind.

So, I jump and punch and run about
And sweat a bucket more
While I tell my wife it would be nice
If she got some ice cream from the store....

CARGO SHORTS

I'm not one to wear short pants
For me it's boots and jeans.
But sometimes in the summer months
It's just too hot it seems.

So I bought some cargo shorts
With pockets everywhere;
They're fairly long and only worn
At home where I don't care

Who might see my pale white legs
That connect me to my feet
That sometimes sport some sandals
To make my outfit complete.

But yesterday it seemed the thing
As I worked out in the yard
To wear those shorts and sandals
While toiling oh, so hard

Beneath the beautiful sky so blue
With high thin clouds above
And of course the crazy wind
That I have grown to "love."

And I kept thinking through the day,
"These shorts ain't too bad!"
They're so much cooler than the jeans
I'm known for since a lad.

But last night when I took a shower
My legs and feet did sting
That until the water hit my hide
Felt fine as anything.

And now I see them red as beets,
Not legs so much as feet,
In funny splotches patterned by
Those sandals and the heat.

And I remember why I don't
Wear shorts out in the sun.
The sunburn there upon my skin
Really isn't fun.

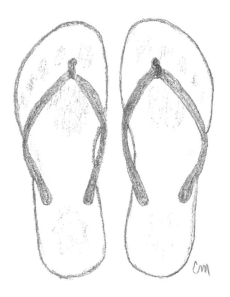

MORNING RITUAL

In goes the water
Then come the grounds
I'm listening to
The percolator sounds.

I smell the aroma
Filling the air
Then sip the first cup
As I sit in my chair.

I take a deep breath
And let out a sigh,
I guess I'll drink coffee
Until the day that I die.

OH, MY ACHING FOOT!

I hurt my foot the other day
Now it's black and blue.
It was because of something stupid
That I knew I shouldn't do.

I was working in the attic
Where it was nice and warm,
Stapling up some insulation
And doing no one harm.

When I came upon a place
Right beside the open door
Where the ladder came right up
From below there on the floor.

I placed a board across the opening,
Just a place on which to stand,
As I hung the insulation
On the wall that was at hand.

And as I was reaching upward
Just as high as I could see
The board I'd placed down under
Seemed no longer to hold me

And I came crashing down
Where my foot hit on the ladder
While the rest of me fell farther
But it could have been much "badder"

For as I was passing through
The hole from which I fell
Both arms caught chunks of lumber
And now don't feel too well.

I guess I should be thankful
For the ladder that was there
'Cause it cushioned me while falling
Through about eight feet of air.

But now I have to fix it
'Cause I guess I'm gaining weight
And the place whereon I hit it
Is now in a broken state.

And my foot just keeps on hurting
Though the swelling has gone down
And I'm too cheap to get it checked
By the doctor here in town.

So, I guess I'll quit complaining'
And hope the pain just goes away
'Cause every time I do I hear,
"Go and get an X-ray!"

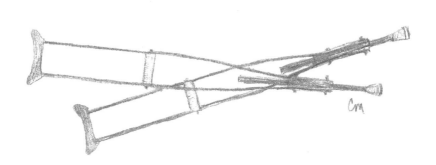

A COLD. BLEH.

Head pounding,
Eyes throbbing,
Lint on my upper lip.

I shoulda shaved this morning
So the Kleenex wouldn't stick.

Dripping,
Aching,
Fever too?

There's nothing here to take
And I don't feel like going to the store.

I hate
A cold
At any time.

I wish we had a warning
When a cold is coming on.

Sneezing,
Coughing,
Droopy eyes.

I'm sure I gave it to everyone
I saw through the holiday.

Sorry about that.

WAITING

Waiting is something
I often do.
I wait for traffic.
I wait for customers.
I wait for the right time.
I wait for inspiration.
I wait for Dinner time.
I wait and wait and wait....

If I wasn't waiting
What would I do?
Would I go fishing?
Then I would wait on the fish to bite.
Would I go shopping?
Then I would wait in line to check out.
Would I watch television?
Then I would wait for the commercial to end.

When will the wait
Ever end?
Not until the Good Lord comes again....

QUIET

I like it quiet.
Perfect silence.
I don't need the noise,
It's just a distraction.

I like it quiet.
I am good with my thoughts.
I don't need the noise,
It just makes me tense.

I like it quiet.
There's nothing to fear.
Most people want noise
To keep them company.

I like it quiet.
It's easier to hear God.
In everyday noise
I can't focus on Him.

I like it quiet.
Especially when I read.
I don't want music playing,
It just pulls me away.

I like it quiet.
Away from the hum
Of the noisy electronics.
They make my head ache.

I like it quiet.
It helps me relax.
Noise just keeps me
From falling asleep…Zzz….

HAIRCUT

This may seem a little strange
But it is on my mind
That sometimes it's the little things
That give sight to the blind.

A haircut is necessity
But when too long without
I feel as though I'm not myself,
In fact, I'm quite the lout.

It seems so simple to sit down
And have them trim my hair
But I hate to have it done at all
So, I avoid the barber chair

Until it can't wait anymore
And force myself, I do
And as the hair piles on the floor
I find myself anew.

CRACKER BARREL SUNDAY

Cracker Barrel
Countrified
Sunday lunch
Fireside

Constant roar
Food aplenty
People talking
Dishes clinking

In from church
Or traveling through
Great Grandma
And babies too

Rich or poor
Suit and tie
Overalls
Satisfied sigh

(This poem was inspired by "Cracker Barrel Old Country Store™")

FRANTICALLY DOING…NOTHING

Don't you just love it when there seems to be
More work than you can possibly do?
When you look at the list of the things to get done
And know that it all falls on you?

Have you noticed how often you almost shut down
When you think of the mountain ahead?
And the great piles of work that are stacked all around
Fill you with nothing but dread?

And you know that you must just dig in and get done
All those things that you know you must do
But distractions abound and those things on the list
Don't get done, but you add something new?

It becomes overwhelming, this growing task list
With scratch-outs, checkmarks and lines
That mark the progress you think you have made
On those chores all entangled like vines.

And isn't it strange at the end of the day
When you take stock of the battles you've won
How your pen full of ink finds no thing to cross off
Because of the list, not a thing has been done?

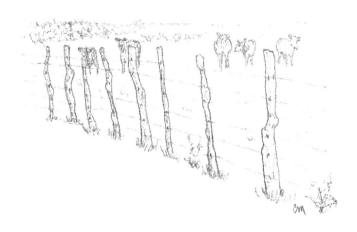

SOMETIMES

Sometimes I'm lazy.
Sometimes I work too hard.

Sometimes I'm creative.
Sometimes I can't get out of my rut.

Sometimes I'm leading.
Sometimes I just want to follow.

Sometimes I'm organized.
Sometimes I can't find anything.

Sometimes I'm at peace.
Sometimes I am on a short fuse.

Sometimes I'm happy.
Sometimes I want to soak in self-pity.

Sometimes I'm consistent.
Sometimes I vacillate from one thing to another.

Sometimes I'm talkative.
Sometimes I need silence.

Sometimes I'm stuck on something.
So, I think I'll make a change....

MUSICALLY CONNECTED

Music inspires
Or can soothe the soul.
It tames the wild beast
Or can rock and roll.

It expresses our heart
Or the thoughts in our mind.
It can lighten our mood
Or cause tears 'til we're blind.

It can tear down the walls
Or, say, "leave me alone."
It can pierce our ear drums
Or be mellower tones.

It can be personal
Or make us part of the crowd.
It can be soft and low
Or, unbearably loud.

It can be background noise
Or the focus of all.
It can be played alone
Or, in a huge music hall.

Music connects
One soul to another;
It crosses all bounds;
Makes us sister and brother.

REPETITION

Have you ever noticed
All the things you do
Are the same as yesterday;
There's not much new?

We get out of bed
Then shower and dress.
Eat a bite
Then spread some stress.

We go to work
Get our coffee cup,
Head down the hall
To fill it up.

We check email
Look at some social book
View our calendar
Then take another look.

Go to meeting one
Then to meeting two.
It's the same old things,
There's nothing new.

Then off to lunch
With the same old crowd.
Head to the local dive
Where it's nice and loud.

The afternoon
Is much the same;
Around and around
It's just a game.

Head home from work,
Do some laundry.
Fix some food
And watch t.v.

Just like Spring,
Summer, Winter and Fall,
The cycle goes;
On a treadmill, all.

I wonder if
We changed something
If the sky would open
And the birds would sing?

We can't expect
A single thing new
If it's all the same,
These things that we do.

COFFEE JITTERS

I like a steaming cup of Joe
To start my every day,
It helps to clear the morning fog
And send me on the way.

Two cups before I head to work
Seems just the thing I need;
One won't do and more than two
Sets my motor to high speed.

But days like this, so wet and cold
Cause me to want to sip
About a gallon of the stuff
At a slow and stately clip.

Then sometime 'long about mid-day
It catches up to me
And I find myself begin to shake
In my extremities.

Wondering what is wrong with me
With head that's all a-buzz
I set my shaking cup right down
And get up to clear the fuzz.

I eat some food and take a break
Trying to clear my head
And find I just can't keep my mind
From wandering instead.

Then along comes the late afternoon
When I am feeling weak,
I crave to fall asleep in bed,
It's all I wish to seek.

Such a toll this humble brew
Wreaks on this body mine,
I swear I'll quit this awful stuff…
But then I smell that smell divine.

THE WORLD IN OUR HAND

Everywhere I look I see people staring at their hand
As though there was something important there to see.
They miss so much around them with their eyes so firmly fixed
I wonder how important it must be!

Maybe it's some kind of window that looks out upon the world
With vistas grand that hold them oh so rapt
Or maybe there's some monster that lurks there within their hand
That has their mind completely in a trap.

I suspect it is the latter if the truth were really known
As to why so many lose their self-control
And focus on the shiny thing that lies within their hand
Even while they're on a quiet country stroll.

DRIPPING

Another Saturday has come around
Bringing its list of chores.
Most of them, it seems today,
Must be done out of doors.

At 6:00 a.m. it's 85
And drips humidity.
Oh, how I dread to go outside
'Cause it's so hard on me.

I'll sweat and sweat and sweat some more
Until I'm wringing wet
And as I walk I'll leave a trail
From all the dripping sweat.

I grew up on the dusty Plains
As dry as it could be
And even when 'twas scorching hot
A breeze was cooling me.

I think I never will get used
To all the moisture in the air
Which just won't seem to fall to ground
That's dry and parched and bare.

How can we be in such a drought
With high humidity?
That water should be doing good
And not afflicting me!

TAKING OUT THE TRASH

This is a poem about something done
A couple of times each week.
It's a chore that comes to everyone,
The high, the low, the meek.

It surely holds some higher truth,
This regular routine
Of taking refuse from the house
That helps to keep it clean.

We're geared up for consumption –
What we wear and what we eat –
And when we're done with using it
We toss it, nice and neat.

It happens with the things we eat,
And all the things we use;
We take just what we need from it,
The rest of it we lose.

So, as you're taking out the trash
Just think, in days of yore
There was no modern plumbing
But a pot behind the door....

Cycling Through the Night

Sometimes in the dark of night
I lie upon my bed
And think on all the many things
That dance within my head.

Of things that I forgot to do
Or things that wait tomorrow
Or things that happened in the day
Or things that cause me sorrow.

My mind is oh, so restless
As I ponder on each thought
And then it shifts unmercifully
To other things unsought.

And I wonder if I'll ever fall
To sleep though hard I try
As I toss and turn about
In my bed there as I lie

Until I wake much later
Not knowing I have slept
But find my thoughts on other things
Which in my mind have leapt.

But for an instant
As I wake and come aware
Of some small noise in the night
That once might give me scare

And I remember dreaming,
Something twisted and confused,
Where thoughts of one thing
With another have been fused.

And so it goes throughout the night.
A pattern soon is seen
Of waking from the depths of sleep,
To dreams of vivid scene.

Until the morning comes and eyes
Become of time aware
That it is the hour of rising
As at the numbers I do stare

And think, "How did my body know
That it was time to be awake
Without alarm clock ringing
Or my shoulder someone shake?"

This body that we dwell within,
Amazing as can be,
Is made so very special
As it seems so plain to me.

And I wonder how one e'er could doubt,
Oh, yes, I find it odd,
That some would ever question
We're made by the Hand of God.

[Sleep cycles intrigue me, and I find it interesting to see how my
Fitbit records them and then compare that to what I remember.
Our minds are amazing things. I rarely use an alarm clock,
but instead decide when I want to awake and almost always
can do so within a minute or two of that time, if not precisely.]

THE BACKYARD BATTLEFIELD

A brilliant tactician,
She seeks the high ground
From which to survey
The battlefield.

Her keen eye glances skyward
To the branches
Which overhang
The lush terrain.

Nostrils slightly flared,
A scent draws her
To look slightly
To her left.

She quietly leaves
Her lofty perch on the planter
To enter a
Stalking crouch.

Movement catches her eye
And she freezes,
Awaiting the coming
Inattention of her prey

Which is focused on finding
An acorn, or
A pecan hiding
In the grass.

The stalk continues
With laser-like intensity,
Always keeping
The tree between

Her line of approach and
The furtive prey
Which occasionally
Sits up to wave

Its bushy tail as if taunting,
Or perhaps,
Warning her that
It is aware of her

Approach across the yard.
The strike comes
Like lightening
And the furry target

Scrambles for the rough bark
That leads it up
And out of reach
Of snapping teeth.

From a branch high above
The chattered scolding
Sounds a challenge
For another day.

RACING TO THE EDGE...

It seems to me that a large percentage of the populace doesn't use
their head. They are easily swayed by television commercials or by
what some celebrity says. They don't spend a lot of time looking into
issues or thinking things through. They just jump on the current
bandwagon and never look back.

The older I get
The less tolerance I have
For people who just won't think.
You know the kind I'm talking about,
They're always agreeing with what you say
With a ready smile and a wink!

It's like they live
With their head in the clouds
And never come down to earth.
They just float along
With the current fad
And praise it for all they are worth.

They never stop
And wonder what
All of the fuss is about.
And if you press them
About what they think
They'll just sit there and pout.

Because that's the problem;
They just haven't thought
About what they're saying so loud.
But they keep on talking
For all that they're worth,
Strutting around so proud.

They just follow the leader
Wherever he goes
Even when it is wrong.
It's like the pied piper

Just marching away
Leading his merry throng.

I like to call them
Lemmings because
They travel around in a crowd.
They rant and rave
And stir up the dust
Just carrying on so loud.

There's just no stopping
This jolly bunch as they
Force their way in a wedge.
They follow their leader
Right up to a cliff
And then right over the edge!

"The fear of the Lord is the beginning of wisdom, and knowledge of the Holy One is understanding." – Proverbs 9:10

VANITY, VISITS, VEXATIONS, VALUES

As I sift through the news,
I see the same old stories
Over and over again. Sometimes the names have been changed
But certainly not to protect the innocent.
It's just like the book of Ecclesiastes where it says
There is nothing new under the sun, It is all vanity.
Even the stories about a country's president,
Who in this post will remain nameless,
That is stirring such a fuss by visiting this country
As a member of the U.N. is not all that new.
What frustrates me is how We play into his hands
By creating a media firestorm over the visit.
All he wants is the spotlight
So that he can tell his oppressed people
How he was such a threat
To the great and powerful U.S.
The same tired faces
Continue to grace the covers
Of so-called news magazines
That focus on their latest scandals or causes
But ignore the real news that continues
Unabated across the globe.
Is it just that people would prefer
To stick their head in the sand
Rather than face the reality
Of war and starvation and genocide
And oppression that never seems to end?
What pursuits are worthy of our treasure?
Where should we invest our time?
What is truly important?
What values are being taught to our children?
Should we care that people are starving in the Sudan?
Does it really matter that a foreign "leader"
Wants to use our media driven culture to stir controversy?
Should we "hole-up" on our shores
And ignore the craziness, or
Should we export that about us which is good
To the rest of the world?

WHAT FOOD CRISIS?

In my wealth, I am concerned
That the price of fuel has increased significantly.

In his poverty, he has no money
To buy the food to feed his children.

If I drove less and bought less
And paid less for the things I desire

Would he have more funds
With which to buy what he needs?

Sadly, no.

In my compassion I give of my plenty
To those who would feed the needy.

Greed siphons the compassionate gift
Until the trickle remaining is almost meaningless.

What is the answer?

One camp says that we should
Redistribute the wealth among the needy.

The other camp says that we should
Teach the needy to feed themselves.

The greedy,
The powerful,
The politicians,
The bureaucrats,

All seek to exploit, pushing their own agenda,
While I continue to worry about the price of fuel
And he still can't feed his family.

TROUBLE AND WORRY

It seems that everywhere you turn
The news is not-so-great.
The world seems to be setting up
To fly apart with hate.

The Middle East continues
In never-ending conflicts
That many think will never end
Until the Good Lord interdicts.

Europe and Asia seem to seethe
With terror and unrest.
Africa is so far gone it can't
Be saved by all the resources of the West.

Here in the United States of America
We're faced with crime and drugs.
It seems our inner cities
Are populated by petty thugs.

Morality is something that
Has fallen in decay
To the same failed thinking
Of the Nihilists in their day.

The bickering in Washington
Is enough to make one sick.
I don't think a complete turnover
Of Congress would even do the trick.

The terrorists are crossing our borders every day,
Prepared to unleash jihad
Until they get their way.

The world my kids and grandkids face
Is one that's filled with gloom.
It makes me wonder sometimes
If they're headed for their doom.

But then I think of Jesus
And how He died upon that tree.

I KNOW THAT IT WILL BE OKAY
Because we have been set free.

"I have told you these things, so that in me you may have peace.
In this world you will have trouble.
But take heart! I have overcome the world." – John 16:33

Nihilism falls into five categories: 1) Existential Nihilism is centered in the thoughts and writings of Nietzsche which contend that all authoritarian structures such as religion are meaningless constructs and that the individual must develop his own set of moral codes. 2) Cosmic Nihilism centers on the insignificance of humanity within the scope of the cosmos. Such insignificance emphasizes that nothing we do really matters so why believe in anything or anyone. 3) Ethical Nihilism is focused on morality. Amoralism is the complete rejection of all moral principles; Egoism is focused purely on self and self-interests with no regard for others; Moral Subjectivism says that we each must develop our own moral code and rejects all authoritarian ethical codes such as religion or government edicts. 4) Epistemological Nihilism claims that knowledge is a false construct based on someone else's views and can never be accepted as fact. 5) Political Nihilism asserts that all political systems are corrupt and should be torn down.

Interestingly, I can identify with some of these viewpoints although not to the extremes of their adherents. I see the need of the individual to develop their own moral code (1) although in my case, I believe it must be based on Biblical principles. I can also see how insignificant we are within the scope of the Cosmos (2); however, I believe that we gain significance through Jesus Christ. I also can see why many ethical systems should be rejected (3) simply because they are either the constructs of men or are tainted by men. Many of our laws concern me in the context of Biblical teaching. I also identify with questioning knowledge (4). I have been involved in too many research projects to simply accept that the proclaimed knowledge of a subject should be taken as fact. Many feel that way about the COVID pandemic. Finally, I also believe that all political systems are corrupt to some extent (5). That doesn't mean they should be torn down in order to construct something new because the new also will be corrupt. There may be times when such rejection is necessary, such as the founding of the United States, but for the most part I believe it is better to work within existing systems.

ELEGANT ELEPHANT

Elegant Elephant wearing pearls
With frills about her waist
Took upon her elegant self
A job much to her taste.

Pretentious Donkey held the throne
Where Elegant wished to sit.
She set upon the lengthy road
In hope of claiming it.

The field was crowded for the feat
As others also vied
To claim the bully pulpit seat
For which she gamely tried.

Her cousins of the elephant clan
Fought hard to claim the prize
And slung such mud upon their quest
They mired her bulky size.

But one by one they all dropped out
As Elegant won the day
To enter on the lofty quest
The public for to sway.

Her tarnished pearls and tattered frills
Were difficult to hide
As voters of most every stripe
The contest would decide.

Finally, the time had come,
The grand election day,
Pretentious versus Elegant,
Which one would get their way?

THE COMMUTE

Blank, staring faces;
Eyes straining in the light;
Hands glued, or drumming,
Or occupied with cell phone,
Coffee, makeup, cigarette,
Or reaching for kids
In their car seats.
Another morning rush-hour
Unfolds to honking horns
And weaving traffic
Because they left too late
To be on time.
It's too bad they can't see
The sunrise splashed
In orange and red and yellow
On the purple-blue of
Fading night,
Or see the hawk
Sitting on the power pole
Watching the madness
Expectantly as if there
Might be flushed a morsel
For his breakfast.
Another day begins.

FRIDAY

In almost every business
There are those who can't wait
For Friday.
They haunt the break room
And their neighbor's cubicle
Talking.
By mid-afternoon
Their productivity goes to zero
And they try to bring
Everyone else
To their level.
How they get by with it
Is anyone's guess.
It could be because
The boss is at
The golf course.

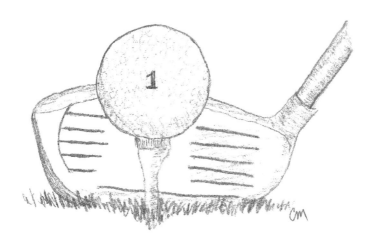

HONEY, WHERE'S THE...?

For much of my career I have worked from a home office. That is probably obvious from many of the things that I have written, but this poem makes it plain that there are sometimes challenges that are rarely faced by those who commute to a workplace office daily.

Upon my desk sit many items,
But mostly there are stacks
Of things not yet completed,
Held for further consideration,
Might be useful later but not yet put away,
Or buried for later discovery.
Near to hand are all these things
Chaotically organized exactly
According to a plan
Known only to me.
Please don't attempt to bring
Order to this mess or I will
Spend weeks trying to find
That one important paper
That I know was right here
That you placed in the proper file
But isn't where I left it!

THE SALESMAN

Over 1,500 miles from home
The master salesman is practicing his art.
He has carefully laid the ground work
By weeks ago, sending out his meticulously prepared material.
It was followed more recently by
A telephone call and a series of emails to set
The ever-important next contact because he knows
That the more contact he can make with you the better his chance.
Calls of confirmation precede the
Culmination of weeks of preparation for the lunch meeting.
Pleasantries are exchanged and past encounters reminded to
Increase the "stickiness" of the meeting so that guards are lowered.
The case of secrets is kept carefully closed
And the items of interest sealed until the meal is consumed
Over questions that probe the needs, desires and situation so that
The pitch can be placed perfectly on the high and inside corner where
Its temptation is greatest.
The competitive situation is assessed while never
Stating anything negative yet always raising questions that say
You are much better than them.
Artfully, the likely objections are dealt with
In the presentation before they are raised
So that they fade into irrelevancy before the final pitch is made.
"Would you be willing to test it for me?"
"I'm sure that any feedback you can provide would be invaluable!"
"If you will just take this on a trial basis, I'm sure you will see
How much improvement it will bring to your operation!"
"There's no risk on your part. How soon can I ship it?"
No product or money are exchanged, but
Agreement is made, and hands are clasped
That the next step in the chain will proceed.
He has done his job well.

AHH, FRIDAY!

Stress accumulates
In the confines of
The office until
Escape becomes
A matter of survival.
That's when the
Springtime weather is
Especially dangerous
Because an avenue
Will be created where
One may not exist
In which to answer
The Siren's song of
Swinging clubs
Upon the links
Or swinging rackets
Upon the courts
Or churning legs
Upon the pedals
Or anything else
Which calls out
"Come to me,
Come to me…."
That is when
The creative side
Flashes its brilliance
With excuses
To answer the call.

SEARCHING

I've dug through heaps of paper
And looked in every drawer
For the one thing that escapes me
That I am looking for.

I know I put it somewhere;
Where that was, I can't recall,
So, I dig and dig and look and look
Until I've found it all
Except what I am looking for.

I thought I had things organized
In folders, nice and straight
Where I could go right to it.
But now it's getting late.
There's piles of things I thought I'd lost
But not what I am looking for.

So, one more time I go right back
To start my search again
In the place that I started,
The book I knew I'd put it in
And what do you know –
It's right there where I put it,
This thing I was looking for!

PRIORITIES

Twenty-six hours in a day
Would help me an awful lot.
The way it is now
The things I want done are not.

I run out of time in the twenty-four hours
Allotted to me every day.
The things that I want to do never fit in
For the have-to-do things in the way!

I spend some time each day
Prioritizing tasks to get done.
But after the tasks are laid out at hand
There's no time left for fun.

If only I had a couple more hours
To be scheduled as time that is free,
I could accomplish the things that I must
And still have time just for me.

But I guess if I'm honest about my wish
It would only be fair to say
I probably couldn't keep my eyes open
For those other two hours in a day.

DETOUR

The couple who are the subject of this post have both passed
on and I wonder what happened to the beautiful place they built.
They were good friends as well as positive examples in our life
at a time we really needed them.

When you move frequently
It is difficult to maintain
Friendships with those
From whom you move away.
It takes effort to maintain
The relationship.
It is always rewarding
But never easy.

Today I made the effort
And it was a wonderful
Side-trip to my travels.
It was only for a couple of hours
But it felt as though the connection
Was renewed and re-energized.

Not only did we visit
But I got the grand tour
Of the new home they are building
That overlooks a beautiful valley
With a creek flowing through.
It is an outstanding site on a hill.
The house is positioned
To maximize the view.
It is uniquely designed
Of native stone
With terraces and a veranda.
I am happy for them.

Some Days

Some days it's hard to know
Whether I'm making progress or not.
It seems that for every step forward
I take two steps back.

Some days it seems
The only progress is in making contact
That perhaps will strengthen a relationship
That with time will grow.

Some days it seems
That there are no right answers
And no wrong answers;
Only choices.

Some days it seems
That all we're doing is sowing
When we want to be reaping.
But it's not time for the harvest.

Some days it seems
That if it wasn't for that one compliment
You would wonder
Why you got out of bed.

Some days it is enough
Just to get through the day
And look back and say,
"At least there were no setbacks."

Do, Doing, Done!

When there is more to do
Of the things you must do
Than you can possibly get done,
How do you do
All the things you must do
In order to ever get done?

It seems there are seasons
For the tasks of this world
That come and go as the spring.
There will be weeks on end
Where the pressure is low
And you don't get wound up about anything.

Then along comes a stretch
Where it all hits the fan
And it seems there is no end in sight.
Everything will pile up
And you can't get it all done
Though you try with all your might.

So, what do you do
When there is more to do
Than you can possibly get done?
Do you just do what you can
And hope for the best
And leave the rest of it undone?

Cell Phone Etiquette

One of the most annoying things
Is for a speaker to be interrupted
By a cellphone going off
In the middle of a presentation.

No, annoying isn't the proper word.
Rude would be a better description.
Sometimes I want to just walk over,
Grab the phone and stomp it to pieces.

Almost every program nowadays
Begins with the admonition
"Please turn all cell phones
And pagers to off or to silent."

And yet, they ring anyway.
No, they don't ring. They blare out
"The Imperial March" from Star Wars,
Or some other personal ringtone.

It's never a quiet ring.
It's always turned as loud as possible –
That's for old folks like me
Who need it turned up to hear it.

It just drives me crazy.
The phone rings,
The speaker pauses,
People look around –

Oops. I guess I forgot to turn mine off....

PATIENT PERSISTENCE

Patient persistence
Leads to progress
While others in a hurry
Temporarily leap ahead
Before being sidelined for their folly.

The lesson could be applied
To business
But I'm talking about
Interstate 40
And a sheet of ice.

Plans and More Plans

Planning is fine –
It must be done, I know.
But nothing is accomplished
Until you get off "Go."

I suppose if you're launching
A ship to the moon,
Each and every detail
Must be in fine tune.

Most earthly projects
Are not so exact
In the requirements
It takes to enact.

It seems that quite often
The course one should take
Isn't quite clear
Until first efforts we make

Are examined.
It is then that we see
Where the course needs adjustment
To get us to where we want to be.

So, go on ahead
And plan details, each one.
While you're doing that
I'll get the job done.

Humming Wheels

The hum of wheels on the highway never ceases
As I sit and watch the commerce of the nation.

Endlessly, the strings of eighteen-wheelers roll by.
Covered with tarps, I guess at the loads they carry.

Some are hauling cattle or other types of stock
And some are hauling containers filled with televisions.

One a moment ago was a tanker full of milk
And now I see a reefer rig hauling ice cream.

They are filled with parts for cars, or cars themselves.
There's loads of gravel and rock for the roads.

I see parts for the giant windmills rising on the plains
And oilfield parts and things that I can't explain.

Loads of corn and food and even fuel
To keep them rolling ever more across this land.

The commerce of the nation is carried on those wheels
That never cease their rolling down the highway.

Thank a truck driver the next time you see one.

THINKING TOWARD PROGRESS

To sit and think
Is sometimes a luxury.
We hurry and rush
From one task to another
Without thinking about
What we are doing or why.

But I've found through the years
That a moment of silence
Reflecting on tasks I must do
Helps me to order
My work for the day
So my efforts will multiply.

It allows me to focus
On what is important
Rather than merely reacting
To whatever crisis
Rears its ugly head
As I go through the course of a day.

So, instead of being pulled
Hither and yon,
Jumping to the whims of others,
I stay on the tasks
That are aimed at my goals
And progress along the way.

CONNECTED

It seems like anymore
I live upon the road
With airplane seats,
Rental cars and
Motels for an abode.

The shape of doing business
Continues to change;
All it takes are laptops
And cell phones
Which allow you to range

All over the country
While managing to attend
To the things that make
Your company grow
Despite the national trend.

The worst part or it all
Is that you can't get away
From work
The way you could
Back in my father's day.

It's with you all the time
No matter where you go
You can always
Be connected
With your laptop and mobile phone!

HIGH FINANCE

Pluses
Minuses
Transpositions

Quickbooks
Checkbooks
Dirty looks

EFT
Paper
Image

Statement
Ledger
Computer

Totaled
Balanced
Reconciled

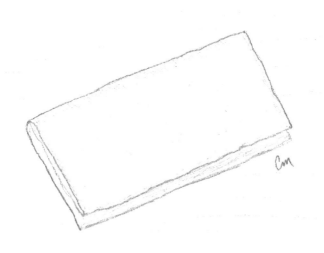

Cell Phone School

I think it is amazing
How cell phone technology
Has become so complicated
For simple guys like me.

I use one in my business
Because of what it lets me do,
Like answer email on the go
And talk to people too.

But I can also surf the web
And then pull up electronic maps
To see where I am going
Or, where I've been, perhaps.

I can even take some pictures
Of the things I do and see
And post them on Social Media
For friends to guess where I might be.

There are lots of applications
I can get upon my cell
Like for making reservations
At a major chain hotel.

I get spreadsheets and reports
Every afternoon at three
That help me know what's going on
At the places I can't be.

There are icons on my phone
That are never even used
Because every time I go to them
I just get more confused.

I wonder what Ma Bell would think
To see what she has done
And how her simple invention
Now does everything under the sun.

I guess it's interesting,
And actually kind of cool,
They now teach you how to use the thing
At a special cell phone school!

LAST MINUTE PREPARATION

Last minute preparation;
Things left undone.
Information undetermined;
Time becomes a gun.

Frantic dispositions
Become the moment's task
While thinking most acutely
Of what we failed to ask.

Have faith my child,
There's naught of fear
That makes a bit of difference
As the date draws near.

Your worry is no matter
In the greater scheme of things;
For it shall be what it becomes
When the fat gal finally sings.

Seeing Without Seeing

Airports and rental cars
Hotels and planes
Torrential downpours
Traveling pains

Eggs for breakfast
Poured from a box
Coffee that tastes
As if brewed from rocks

City to city
And coast to coast
Of the places I've been
There are many to boast

But often they pass
As if lacking a name
Because after a while
They all look the same

ANOTHER AIRPORT

If I recall correctly, this was written on my cell phone as a Blog post while sitting in the airport in Greenville, South Carolina. It was not long afterward that I turned in my resignation.

Blue skies beckon through the pane
O'er hills all cloaked in trees.
Another week has come and gone
As Corporate gods I please.

I bounce around across this land
Once home to Liberty,
As those in power do all they can
Enslaving those once free.

I wonder why I work so hard
For something with no soul
When all they ever ask is more
To meet their looming goal?

For Corporate gods and Washington
Are working hand in hand
To make us bow to greed and power
In this and every land.

Disillusioned, tired, and bent
I sit and wait again
For shining bird to take me home
One night to rest and then

Once more, I face the winding road
With work that's never done,
Aiming for those fleeting goals
While all the while the sun

Shines on mountains, distant, blue,
Home to certain peace;
A place of refuge not too far –
Escape from this mad race.

But no, I get upon the plane
Just two short legs away
From one who waits alone at home
Wishing I could stay.

If only that was what I could
But it will never be;
I'll suck it up and do my job
For those who depend on me.

Reflecting as I sit and brood
A calmness dwells in me.
I know that it is God alone
Sustaining all I see

Out window clear and sky so blue
And there He speaks to me
That peace and rest reside in Him
And only there I'm free

Living out His Grand Design,
For He has called me here,
Staring into distant blue
Stuck in this airport drear

Reflecting on the life I live
With hardly time at home
Where I would sit and rest awhile
Never more to roam.

OH, WHAT IF I AM WRONG?

Sometimes making decisions
Of the highly consequential kind
Can drive a wedge of fear
Into the unwary mind.

It's the fear of consequences
That might occur should I be wrong.

But fear can often bind us
From reaching for the stars.
It binds us to forever stand
Within these earthly bars.

Instead, we wring our hands and cry,
"Oh, what if I am wrong?!"

While swirling about our throbbing head
Opportunities pass us by
That would exceed our expectations
If only we would try.

So, blind from indecision
For fear of being wrong,

We fret and worry over things
That never will come true
If we'll just shoulder to the plow
And join the mighty few

Who soar above the moaning crowd
That fear they might be wrong.

TRAVEL AND WORK

When I travel for my work I find the hours are mighty long.
I work when I awake and often well into the night.

The phone is always ringing, this computer in my hand
That buzzes with the email or when a text the screen does light.

Instead of setting it aside to wait until the 'morrow
I frequently just deal with it and sometimes work quite late.

For what else am I going to do while stuck in a hotel
Since I care not for the t.v. where mindless heads do prate?

I usually fill the silence with a keyboard in my hand
And if by chance I find the time I often sit and write;

It is a simple thing that can occupy my mind
Even if it's something like this poem I wrote last night.

MY DESK

It seems I have a messy desk.
I must admit it's so.
But everything that rests on it
Is in a place I know.

It is a desk quite large you see
And there is lots of space
That would likely go to waste
Without these things in place.

For otherwise I'd have to dust,
Not something that I do
Too willingly it seems,
At least as I've been told, so

I use it to keep organized
The projects that I'm on
With one stack here, another there,
Another over yon

Beside the pottery shards
Picked up out on our place
Beneath the shelf that holds the statue
With the Incan face.

And by the cup that holds the pens,
There is a stack of cards.
That is just the least of them
For I have them in yards

Stuffed in a drawer. From ages past,
They're likely worthless now
But there's surely a good reason
I hang onto them somehow.

And there are several yellow pads
Each one with different things
Written on the pages there
And to them often clings

A sticky note that I have placed
To mark a certain spot,
Or, maybe just to emphasize
Some written, special thought.

And up above, on the top shelf,
Mementos of the past
Or, pictures that the grandkids drew,
The things I want to last.

And of course, there on the floor
Rests a box or two
Or, three or, four or maybe more
That lean somewhat askew.

But, I know what is in each place
And filed within my mind
Is a virtual map of things
I could find even if blind

And if you try to clean my desk
By moving things around
I would be quite upset with you
For things that would ne'er be found.

WRITING

As the brush is
To canvas
The pen is
To paper
And in the hand
Of the Master,
Wonder unfolds.

COMMENTS

With the pervasiveness of social media comes the inevitable divisiveness that is exacerbated by comments made on the posts of others. Electronic anonymity seems to erase manners and often, common sense, or any sense at all. Some feel they must comment on everything that is posted no matter how well, or how little they know the subject, or the one doing the posting. Opinions are "cheap" these days. That situation inspired the following:

I usually find it easy
To comment on someone's work,
But I know sometimes in doing so
I come off like a jerk.

It isn't my intention
To be so critical;
It's just that my mind
Is highly analytical.

When I read what has been written
And I find I can't agree,
The thoughts go into overdrive
And manners sometimes flee.

It's not meant to be belittling
Or to cause a fight,
But when I can't agree with you
It's because I know I'm right!

182

THE DESERT

I am dry.
Lost in the desert
Of my imagination,
I trudge toward the shimmering
Thoughts that dance before me
Only to find bare sand.

The well,
The never-dry fount
That pours forth upon request,
Has been erased
From the map.
It is gone.

Always
I had but to begin
The journey and the spring
Welling deep inside
Poured forth the clear
Pure words,

But not today.
Today the sand stretches
As far as I can see
In every direction.
Tantalizing with
Mirages.

Yet I trudge on;
Putting one foot
In front of the other
Until the page
Is no longer
Blank.

PREDATOR

In the depths of the Kalahari of far Africa
Lives a wild dog.
It is painted in such a way that it blends
With the environment.
It is a cooperative animal that runs in packs
To hunt large ungulates.
It's prey is often much more massive than this small
Beast that isn't truly a dog, but acts like one
Except that it is not easily tamed.

I think the African Wild Dog would make a good politician.
It understands how to pick off the vulnerable
And has no qualms about exploiting the quietly grazing
Population who could rise up and defeat their
Pernicious attacks if only they would band together.
It must be a universal trait of all living things
To turn away and sigh, "at least it wasn't me this time."

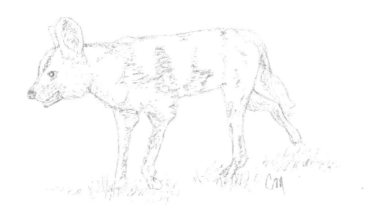

FORGETFULNESS

It seems occasionally I
Have flashes of inspiration,
Insights worthy of saving
For some future generation.

They frequently seem to happen
At times most inopportune,
Like two o'clock in the morning
When I should be snoring a tune.

You'd think after all of this time
I would have learned to prepare
And keep a pad a pencil
On my bedside table there.

But no, I think I'll remember
Anything worthy of claim,
But when I wake in the morning
I can barely remember my name!

JUST SOME WORDS

As previously mentioned, much of the work presented in this collection were originally blog posts. The discipline of posting something daily was often a struggle for me. This poem was an attempt to describe that struggle on a particular day when the words just wouldn't come easily. I did manage to be a little creative in the use of punctuation. That's one of the fun things about poetry, along with the fact that it doesn't necessarily have to rhyme, the punctuation can be creative as well.

I ramble
I digress
I can't think!
What a mess.

Gotta focus
Much to do
Get organized!
So, what's new?

Get prepared
Lock it down
Finish up!
Lose the frown.

It ain't that hard
Just speak your mind
Open up!
Don't act so blind.

It's just a post
Just messing 'round
Type some words!
You're NOT profound!!

HERDING CATS

I have a friend named Neal who introduced me to the phrase,
Herding cats.
It certainly evokes an image in your mind about how it might
Be difficult.
I've always preferred to have my
Ducks in a row.
It requires much less effort and has a more
Predictable result.
Getting one's ducks in a row
Takes leadership.
Have you ever noticed how the ducklings all line up
Behind momma?
Herding cats, on the other hand, is a maneuver best executed
From behind.
That implies one is at least attempting to manage
The unmanageable.
It's so much better when it just happens naturally like with
Brown pelicans.
They just seem to line up and ride the breeze
While I watch.

No Silence Found Here

Sometimes when I seek
A quiet place of peace,
I struggle with the sounds
That seem to never cease.

The television plays
In a room that's much too near
And the hum of electronics
Is forever in my ear.

All I want is silence
In which to contemplate
The things of this day's passage
Before it gets too late

So, here I sit composing,
Seeking that which is profound,
But my thoughts are disconnected
And just go round and round.

I think if it was quieter
I could likely do much more,
But then there in the quietness
I might just close my eyes and snore.

THE MISSION

The creak of wooden carreta wheels lulls the trudging, weary travelers
As they move slowly across the shimmering heat of the trackless
Wilderness filled with thorns and rocks.
Their belief in the work of bringing enlightenment
to ignorant savages
Draws them onward against great odds into a land of Pueblos
Filled with people who have long inhabited this high desert.
By whatever means necessary, they adhere to their task,
Whether through education, or force, or even death to those
Who would not submit to their creed.
It is a corruption of the very gospel they seek to serve that they
Use the tools of darkness to bring light to those who
Welcomed them into their home with open arms.
Dogma replaced faith and the generations who descend
From those who survived the destruction continue
In adherence to the tenants taught their ancestors.
Despite the darkness so long ago inflicted,
Shimmers of light peek through the lives and hearts
Of those who found the truth beneath.

Words On a Page

Sometimes when I sit and think,
Or look at a blank page,
I wonder why I take the time to write.

Instead, I could just take a nap,
Or sit and drink a cup,
And in the peaceful moment take delight.

I feel compelled it seems
To put word to page,
Recording there the things that fill my mind.

Is it some gremlin in my head
That's bent to waste my time?
Or are there reasons I have yet to find

That drive me to apply my fingers
To the plastic keys
And watch the words that scroll across the screen

That sometimes seem so simple
And at other times complex?
While most of them are likely never seen

By anyone but me who cares
One whit about what I write
Especially when they're as they are today,

Where they are just a sequence of
Black letters on the page
And nothing there important to say.

RARE

There are moments in life that are special.
They stand against the panoply of time.
Though attacked by the insults that never seem to end
Those moments last.

We must cherish those moments as something rare
That requires our protection.
They become a source of strength and peace
That pulls us through difficulties which seem to never end.

Just a Short One

There are times of the day when my head starts to nod,
So, I get up and just walk around.
It gets the old blood to working again
And my energy seems to rebound.

But then there are times, like right after lunch,
When a walk just doesn't quite work.
I find myself nodding deeper and deeper
Until I awake with a jerk.

Perhaps it's a snort that wakes me right up
Or maybe the drool on my chin,
That makes me look and see who had seen
What caused my sheepish grin.

The best thing to do is to sit in my chair
And lean back with my sleepy eyes closed,
Until I awake refreshed and renewed
Knowing that I have just dozed.

THE FAR HORIZON

I wonder, sometimes, what's over the hill
Where my eyes can't quite see?
It's part of the restless nature I guess
That seems to reside in me.

It's as though there's a Siren that calls to my mind
That nobody else can hear.
It draws my eye to the far horizon
Rather than focus on that which is near.

I think it's a part of the way I am wired
That causes my heart to roam
Or maybe it's just that deep down inside
I know that this place isn't home.

(Jim Reeves wrote the song, "This World is Not My Home," which
begins with the words, "This world is not my home I'm just a-passing
through, my treasures are laid up somewhere beyond the blue."
Perhaps that is why I am always looking beyond the horizon....)

Defense

Along the pathways
We often find
Things of beauty
That God designed.

A beautiful flower
Stands lily white
To scent the air
And delight our sight.

It draws the bee
To pollen there
But dare not touch
This sight so fair

For it is wreathed
About with thorns
To prick the hands
Like tiny horns.

Dare not touch
It where it lies,
Just drink its beauty
With your eyes.

More Words on a Page

Words written on a page
Are windows
Into that
Which lies beyond
Our own experience.

We learn,
We imagine,
We live
The words.

In them we may see
The pathways
Not traveled
And find enlightenment
For our needs.

We learn,
We imagine,
We live
The words.

It may be the "how to,"
Or a biography,
Or it might be
A flight of fancy
That provides escape.

We learn,
We imagine,
We live
The words.

They provide insight
Into that which
Went before,
Or perhaps a glimpse
Of what lies ahead.

We learn,
We imagine,
We live
The words.

Through recorded experience,
We learn.
Through recorded conjecture,
We imagine.
By embracing the written word,
We expand our lives.

INDEX OF POEMS

Miscellaneous

Nature/Outdoors

People

Politics

Weather/Seasons

Western

Work

INDEX OF ILLUSTRATIONS

Printed in the USA
CPSIA information can be obtained
at www.ICGtesting.com
JSHW012130240924
70158JS00003B/7